OVERCOMING
EATING DISORDERS

OVERCOMING EATING DISORDERS

ROBERT S. M^CGEE

W M. DREW MOUNTCASTLE, M. A., L. P. C.

Rapha Publishing/Word, Inc.
Houston and Dallas, TX

Rapha's Twelve-Step Program for Overcoming Eating Disorders
by Robert S. McGee and Wm. Drew Mountcastle

Unless otherwise indicated, Scripture quotations are from the NEW AMERICAN STANDARD BIBLE, © The Lockman Foundation, 1960, 1962, 1963, 1968, 1971, 1972, 1973, 1975, 1977.

Scripture quotations noted NIV are taken from the HOLY BIBLE: NEW INTERNATIONAL VERSION. Copyright © 1973, 1978, 1984 International Bible Society. Used by permission of Zondervan Bible Publishers.

The Twelve Steps have been reprinted and adapted with permission from Alcoholics Anonymous World Services, Inc., to extend to all persons suffering from eating disorders, and to credit the One whom we believe is our source of power: Jesus Christ.

Portions of *The Search for Significance* book and workbook reprinted and adapted by permission. Robert S. McGee (2d ed. Copyright © 1990 by Robert S. McGee; Houston and Dallas, TX: Rapha Publishing/Word, Inc.)

Portions of *Rapha's Twelve-Step Program for Overcoming Chemical Dependency* reprinted and adapted by permission. Robert S. McGee, with Pat Springle and Susan Joiner. 2d ed. Copyright © 1990 Rapha Publishing; Houston and Dallas, TX: Rapha Publishing/Word, Inc.

Rapha's Twelve-Step Program for Overcoming Eating Disorders represents the experiences and opinions of Rapha and the authors. Opinions expressed herein are not to be attributed to Alcoholics Anonymous as a whole, nor does *Rapha's Twelve-Step Program for Overcoming Eating Disorders* imply any endorsement by Alcoholics Anonymous.

Fourth Printing, 1992
ISBN: 0-945276-19-2
Printed in the United States of America

To the staff of the Rapha Program,
Hill Country Hospital, San Antonio, TX:

James F. Jennings, M.D.,
because every ship needs her captain;

And to:

Wence
Sue
Dale
Lisa
Wendell

Also to:

Cliff
Joyce

And, of course, to
Valerie
and her "real workers"

And to Pat, Susan and Sandy,
who contributed to the production of this workbook:
The road is long and hard, not easy but simple,
and opportunities can be fun (Eccles. 4:9-12).

And to all Rapha therapists everywhere,
who are treating eating disorders and so much more:
Heb. 11:38a
You daily demonstrate to those who come seeking that
they, too, are "people of infinite worth . . . "

The Twelve Steps of Alcoholics Anonymous*

1. We admitted we were powerless over alcohol—that our lives had become unmanageable.
2. Came to believe that a Power greater than ourselves could restore us to sanity.
3. Made a decision to turn our will and our lives over to the care of God *as we understood Him.*
4. Made a searching and fearless moral inventory of ourselves.
5. Admitted to God, to ourselves, and to another human being the exact nature of our wrongs.
6. Were entirely ready to have God remove all these defects of character.
7. Humbly asked Him to remove our shortcomings.
8. Made a list of all persons we had harmed, and became willing to make amends to them all.
9. Made direct amends to such people wherever possible, except when to do so would injure them or others.
10. Continued to take personal inventory and when we were wrong promptly admitted it.
11. Sought through prayer and meditation to improve our conscious contact with God *as we understood Him,* praying only for knowledge of His will for us and the power to carry that out.
12. Having had a spiritual awakening as the result of these steps, we tried to carry this message to alcoholics, and to practice these principles in all our affairs.

---

* From *Alcoholics Anonymous*, 3d ed. (New York: World Services, 1976), 59-60. Reprinted here and adapted on the following pages by permission from A.A. World Services, Inc. Permission to reprint and adapt the Twelve Steps does not mean that A.A. has revised or approved the content of this workbook, nor that A.A. agrees with the views expressed herein. A.A. is a program of recovery from alcoholism. Use of the Twelve Steps in connection with programs and activities which are patterned after A.A. but which address other problems does not imply otherwise.

Contents

We admit that by ourselves we are powerless over our eating behaviors—that our lives have become unmanageable. *For I know that nothing good dwells in me, that is, in my flesh; for the wishing is present in me, but the doing of the good is not* (Rom. 7:18).

We come to believe that God, through Jesus Christ, can restore us to sanity . . . . *for it is God who is at work in you, both to will and to work for His good pleasure* (Phil. 2:13).

We make a decision to turn our lives over to God through Jesus Christ. *I urge you therefore, brethren, by the mercies of God, to present your bodies a living and holy sacrifice, acceptable to God, which is your spiritual service of worship* (Rom. 12:1).

We make a searching, courageous moral inventory of ourselves. *Let us examine and probe our ways, and let us return to the Lord* (Lam. 3:40).

We admit to God, to ourselves and to another person the exact nature of our wrongs. *Therefore, confess your sins to one another, and pray for one another, so that you may be healed* (James 5:16a).

We commit ourselves to God, desiring that He remove patterns of sin from our lives. *Humble yourselves in the presence of the Lord, and He will exalt you* (James 4:10).

We humbly ask God to renew our minds so that our sinful patterns of behavior can be transformed into patterns of life and health and righteousness. *And do not be conformed to this world, but be transformed by the renewing of your mind, that you may prove what the will of God is, that which is good and acceptable and perfect* (Rom. 12:2).

We make a list of all persons we have harmed, and become willing to make amends to them all. *And just as you want men to treat you, treat them in the same way* (Luke 6:31).

We make direct amends to such people where possible, except when doing so will injure them or others. *If therefore you are presenting your offering at the altar, and there remember that your brother has something against you, leave your offering there before the altar, and go your way; first be reconciled to your brother, and then come and present your offering* (Matt. 5:23-24).

We continue to take personal inventory, and commit to agree with the truth about ourselves and act upon it. *Therefore let him who thinks he stands take heed lest he fall* (1 Cor. 10:12).

We learn to grow in our relationship with Jesus Christ through prayer, meditation and obedience, seeking His wisdom and power to live according to His will as He reveals it to us. *But if any of you lacks wisdom, let him ask of God, who gives to all men generously and without reproach, and it will be given to him. But let him ask in faith without any doubting, for the one who doubts is like the surf of the sea driven and tossed by the wind* (James 1:5-6).

Having had a spiritual awakening, we try to carry the message of Christ's grace and restoration power to others with eating disorders, and to practice these principles in all of our affairs. *All this is from God, who reconciled us to himself through Christ and gave us the ministry of reconciliation . . . and he has committed to us the message of reconciliation. We are therefore Christ's ambassadors, as though God were making his appeal through us* (2 Cor. 5:18, 19b, 20, NIV).

Introduction

What are "eating disorders"?

Let's begin by establishing what eating disorders are not.

Eating disorders are not the strange food cravings women may experience during pregnancy. Eating disorders are not personal habits of overeating with consequential weight gains, nor are they necessarily the habits of skipping meals with consequential weight loss. An eating disorder is not the inability to stick to a diet. Eating disorders are not those strange food-related behaviors which usually accompany borderline personality disorder, in which eating-disorder-like behavior occurs as part of a spectrum of self-destructive acts, such as self-mutilation, substance abuse and suicide attempts.

So what *are* eating disorders?

Specifically, eating disorders are compulsive-addictive behavioral patterns in which a person's substance of choice for abuse is food. Eating disorders divide into four main categories:

A. *Anorexia Nervosa:* Literally, "nervous lack of appetite," a misnomer. Originally referenced as "nervous consumption" and "anorexia hysterica," anorexia nervosa is simply addictive dieting, deliberate self-starvation, comprising one part of the compulsive drive for perfection and control common to all addictions.

B. *Bulimia Nervosa:* Literally, "ox hunger." Bulimic-like behavior may be seen as a symptom of anorexia nervosa, but bulimia nervosa stands alone as a distinctive eating disorder. Bulimia is characterized by intensive, secretive patterns of *binge-eating* (rapid consumption of high-calorie, sugary, fatty foods, or high-fiber, watery vegetables, such as salads); followed by expedient *purging*, or elimination, of the food consumed during the binge. This is accomplished by self-induced vomiting, laxative and/or diuretic abuse or excessive and compulsive exercise in which the goal is to "get rid of everything quick." Bulimia is supported by convoluted and confused emotional reactions to a dysfunctional relationship with one or both parents (most often, an enmeshed relationship in which at least one parent is emotionally dependent, overly-controlling and/or sexually abusive).

C. *Compulsive Overeating:* Overeating which resembles bulimic-like binging (which may or may not be secretive) or "grazing" over a period of hours with the intent of escaping or anesthetizing feelings of anger, inadequacy, humiliation, fear, loneliness, boredom or other unwelcome emotions. Rapid weight gains are the result, since no purgative behavior accompanies the binge.

D. *Pica:* The most rare of the eating disorders. Pica is the pathological eating of non-nutritive substances—dirt and excrement, for example.

Why do eating disorders occur?

An eating disorder may result from a number of likely and plausible causes, all of which vary with the individual. Two key emotional and spiritual components, however, inaugurate and sustain all eating disorders: *perfectionism* and *control*. These components are reinforced by an almost non-existent self-esteem. Usually, people with eating disorders have no concept of being loved and accepted unconditionally. For this reason, they rely on ego defenses that effectively envelop and protect their fragile self-concepts and identities, looking to another person—a parent, spouse, child, teacher, clergy member—to provide the love and acceptance they need. Their relationships thus may be characterized by one or more of the following:

• *Emotional Dependency:* A strongly-held belief that emotional stability and fulfillment can only be obtained by clinging persistently to a strong, nurturing person. This clinging may appear to be passive, benign and even endearing ("I need you so much . . . how did I ever get along without you?"), or chaotic, desperate and sometimes threatening ("If you leave me, I can't go on living . . . I'll just kill myself!"). At the root of emotional dependency are an irresponsibility for personal growth and development, and an infantile need for nurturing and security through a strong, adult-like figure who must never leave.

- *Isolation:* As Americans, we seem to have a passion for the rugged, strong, "Lone-Ranger" individualist, who is self-assured and self-reliant, and maintains a safe distance from the emotional entanglements of others. Distance seems to guarantee protection from the possibility of hurt. It is not surprising, then, that those who have been deeply hurt isolate themselves from others—emotionally and geographically—as a means of self-protection. However, such isolation carries with it its own pain, which the person then seeks to deaden through any number of compulsive behaviors, sometimes including an eating disorder.

- *Codependency:* Codependency is a compulsion to control and rescue people by fixing their problems. It occurs when a person's God-given needs for love and security have been blocked in a relationship with a primary dysfunctional person, resulting in a lack of objectivity, a warped sense of responsibility, being controlled and controlling others, and in hurt and anger, guilt, and loneliness.[1]

  With an eating disorder, codependent behavior typically is played out in one of two ways. In some cases, those who either cannot or will not take responsibility for themselves will seek out the seemingly omni-competent, overly-responsible codependent, whose gratification comes from rescuing and taking care of others. In other cases, those who attempt to compensate for their unmet needs by resorting to eating-disordered behavior may also be codependent. Eating-disordered behavior gives them the illusion that they are self-nurturing, and protects them from exposing their weaknesses to others, especially those for whom they are "so responsible."

These defenses, along with approval-seeking and other unhealthy styles of interaction with others, reflect the eating-disordered person's personal attempts to control the chaotic instability and pain of his or her life. Failure is no deterrent; the eating-disordered person just tries to perform more perfectly, accomplish more results and work even harder at pleasing others. *Surely if I just try harder, the world will be all right and I will be happy!* he or she believes. Such thinking is self-centered and is doomed to failure for at least two reasons: (1) None of us is God; therefore, we cannot rearrange the universe; (2) As a result of our efforts to gain acceptance and approval by our performance, others will accept our performance, not us. We always will be several paces behind the very acceptance we seek!

Still, eating-disordered persons keep plugging away, expending great emotional energy to rein in, perfectly control and submerge their emotional responses—especially anger, personal hurt and loneliness—and to always be the perfect, socially correct, unassuming, self-giving, attending models of "nice" people. They will be people-pleasing examples of self-sacrifice and nobility, using isolation and secrecy both to hide their eating-disordered behavior and to make sure no one gets close enough to see the falseness of their perfectionistic facades.

On the surface, it may seem ironic that people with addictions like eating disorders suffer from low self-esteem and yet tenaciously rely on their own personal defense mechanisms to maintain control over their lives. But a further examination of human nature since the Fall (Genesis 3) reveals that we have exchanged the self-esteem that is based on being God's image-bearers for that which makes our value and worth dependent on our performance and the approval of others. This latter way of thinking results in our becoming perfectionistic, manipulative, secretive and controlling to earn "our place in the sun," to make sure that our performance is above criticism and to project the appearance that "all is well" and thereby maintain the approval of others.

It is for these reasons that recovery from eating disorders requires two very important tools: *honesty* and *openness*. Meeting these requirements often is best accomplished in a group setting with others who have eating disorders, and who also recognize that secrecy and isolation are an eating disorder's closest allies.

People with eating disorders also generate and maintain personal defenses to replace their violated emotional boundaries. To avoid responding in an outwardly unfavorable manner to the anger, pain, stress, hopelessness, weaknesses and fears of others, they absorb these emotional expressions. The anorexic does so by attempting to "fade away" in order that such feelings might be removed forever. The bulimic stuffs and violently purges the anger and resentment of being the emotional switchboard of a dysfunctional family system. The compulsive overeater stuffs and medicates strong feelings by shoving down large amounts of fattening foods into his or her system. Because of the strains which eating disorders exact on a person's internal organs, biochemistry and hormone levels, eating disorders must be understood as health- and life-threatening addictions. The emotional dynamics and convoluted thought patterns which accompany these disorders present sometimes insurmountable roadblocks to mature, healthy, growing relationships with significant others.

There is hope for the person with an eating disorder: spiritual hope. One cannot be free from the problem through willpower and self-control. A person with an eating disorder has a relationship with food in which food controls the person; the person therefore cannot control the food-related behavior by exercising more willpower or self-effort. However, the eating-disordered person can exercise *responsibility,* a major component in recovery. Initial responsibility requires following these basic but essential steps:

- Admitting, *I have a problem which I cannot control; rather, it is controlling me.*
- Acknowledging, *Someone* (God)*has the power I lack to save me, and I am not Him!*
- Deciding, *I can place my life in the hands of a loving God, who desires to help me and intervene on my behalf, and allow Him to manage my affairs.*
- Consenting to major life-changes to replace the thinking and behaviors which have supported the eating disorder (in part, working the Twelve Steps).
- Seeking fellowship with others who are afflicted by eating disorders in a program of recovery.
- Consenting to medical/dietetic management of food intake and dietary habits, with a release of control and fear surrounding body image, weight and caloric consumption. (This may necessitate inpatient treatment in a hospital, or at least outpatient therapy and counseling.)

For the eating-disordered person, it is important to understand that our goal in recovery is *progress*, not perfection. The ongoing process for effective, lasting change has four components: cognitive, relational, spiritual and temporal.

Cognitive: As you gain a better understanding of your background, feelings and thoughts, and the truths found in God's Word (the Bible), you will be able to apply specific biblical truths to your deepest needs, hurts and desires.

Relational: As we already have mentioned, fellowship is vital to recovery. Personal reflection and application are most effective in an environment of affirmation and encouragement. It is extremely difficult— if not impossible—to overcome the painful causes and effects of an addictive disorder alone. You need the support of others who have gone through (and are going through) this program of healing. This is especially important! Often those closest to us, though they may mean well, have learned that our repeated promises to stop our compulsive behaviors mean nothing. They now may be understandably dubious that this time, we mean business. Those who have been where you are now understand. Let them help you!

Spiritual: As you examine God's truths and begin to experience His forgiveness and strength, you will grow in your understanding of His character and purposes in your life. You also will gain a new attitude about accepting others and sharing yourself with them.

Temporal: Again, recovery is a process. Lasting change will not occur overnight. You may experience flashes of insight occasionally, but the process of real growth is long, slow and steady. Expecting too much too soon may cause you to become disillusioned, and pull out of the program altogether. Be patient. Work through the exercises in this workbook carefully. Growth and health will come . . . gradually.

Perhaps you do not feel the need to exercise the responsibilities we've outlined because you do not see yourself as having an eating disorder to begin with. Perhaps you do not see your binging and purging as an unmanageable problem, your reluctance to eat as anorexic self-starvation or your grazing as hurtful. Fair enough. But if others are giving you feedback that your behavior and appearance are indicative of a problem, they may not be completely wrong. You will need to work the first of the Twelve Steps to assess your condition. If you then conclude that you have an eating disorder, you will be ready for the second step, and so on. In all of this, you will find relentless honesty and openness with others and yourself to be your faithful and true allies and friends. Without them, recovery is impossible.

May God bless your journey, step by step, beginning with the first, all-important step.

*About the Twelve Steps . . .**

Twelve-Step groups—and their related books, pamphlets and other materials—are the legacy of Alcoholics Anonymous (A.A.), self-described as:

> . . . a fellowship of men and women who share their
> experience, strength and hope with each other that they
> may solve their common problems and help others to recover
> from alcoholism. The only requirement for membership is a
> desire to stop drinking. There are no dues or fees for A.A.
> membership; we are self-supporting through our own
> contributions. A.A. is not allied with any sect,
> denomination, politics, organization, or institution;
> does not wish to engage in any controversy;
> neither endorses nor opposes any causes.
> Our primary purpose is to stay sober and help other
> alcoholics achieve sobriety.[2]

Since 1935, the fellowship of Alcoholics Anonymous has been a door to sobriety, freedom and sanity for many alcoholics who were powerless in the face of their addiction. The simplicity of the Twelve Steps and Twelve Traditions has been adapted into other groups, such as AlAnon, AlaTeen, Narcotics Anonymous and Overeaters Anonymous, among others, all of which focus on a desperate desire to escape the terror of compulsive, addictive behavior, and find regeneration and restoration in their lives and relationships. Many have achieved these goals by working through the Twelve-Step program, and thus have been able to live fruitful, productive lives.

Unfortunately, the Twelve Steps and related programs of recovery have come under sharp criticism in Christian circles due to their vague, spiritual emphasis which does not stress freedom in Jesus Christ, but in a "Power greater than ourselves" and "God *as we understood Him*." Because of this wording, many Christians have chosen to abandon the Twelve Steps altogether. Ironically, in addition to cutting themselves off from a powerful and successful tool for recovery, these people have re-created the very reason why A.A. was not, from its beginning, a Christian group.

Alcoholics Anonymous was the brainchild of William G. Wilson, who has become known to millions of alcoholics as "Bill W." Wilson was born in 1895 in the small town of East Dorset, Vermont. His father was an alcoholic who left his young family in 1905, not to have any contact with them again until 1914. His mother became a physician.

Although young Bill was well-warned of the pitfalls and shame attached to alcohol, he began his drinking career as a doughboy in Europe during World War I. When he returned to the States in 1918, he married Lois Burnham and embarked on a plan which he believed would win them good fortune. He would hitch-hike onto the post-war economic prosperity that was sweeping the victorious, isolationist nation by traveling around the country to visit growing industries. In the process, he would speculate on their growth by talking with factory workers as they got off work, pumping them for information with liberal amounts of speakeasy booze, and then phone back his valuable information to traders on Wall Street.

Packing his bride into the side-car of a Harley-Davidson motorcycle, Bill traveled the country on his quest, camping by the roadside, progressively drinking more and producing less. The stock market crash of 1929 brought an end to industrial development and to Bill's travels, but not to his drinking. Arriving back in New York, Bill and Lois eventually had to move in with her father, a physician who had little tolerance for Bill's drinking and its effects on Lois, as well as the embarrassments it caused the entire family.

After a time, Bill went to see William Silkworth, M.D. Dr. Silkworth had a high interest in alcoholism and its effects, and most importantly, a compassion for its victims. Dr. Silkworth noted Bill's physical deterioration and warned him that he must stop drinking. This led to hospital detoxification on several occasions, all of which ended the same way: Bill would return to drinking. Since he was in no shape to be the breadwinner, Lois became responsible for their income. Meanwhile, Bill continued to make promises that he would stop drinking, and continued to drink.

Then, in November, 1934, Bill received a call from an old drinking buddy, Ebby Thacher. Many and hazardous had been their inebriated adventures, and Bill fondly welcomed this contact. When Thacher arrived to call on his old friend, Bill, the genteel host, was already half-drunk and had a bottle and glass to share. When he offered a drink to Thacher, the response he received was far from expected: Ebby Thacher refused a drink! Bill noticed that his friend's posture was erect and that his face was not care-worn and heavy with the deterioration of a terminal alcoholic, like his own. When Bill queried Thacher on this, the response again was unexpected—and not altogether welcomed: "Bill, I got religion!"

Thacher had become sober and had maintained his sobriety as the result of a "spiritual awakening" and participation in a society called the "Oxford Group," which had been founded in the 1920s by Frank Buchman, a Lutheran pastor and evangelical lecturer. The group was comprised of non-sectarian Christians whose goal was a "God-guided life" emphasized by fellowship through informal gatherings, self-examination and mutual support and encouragement, among other things. Buchman's ministry was primarily directed toward the ne'er do well of the day.

While the movement was still gaining momentum, an alcoholic named Rowland H. sought treatment from a Swiss psychiatrist named Carl Gustav Jung. Jung told Rowland that the only thing that could save him was a "spiritual awakening." Belief in God was not enough, Jung told him. A "vital experience" was required and might be found through an alliance with a religious group.

Rowland heard about the Oxford Group, was impressed by its simple teachings and became a member. It was Rowland who carried the message to Thacher, who in turn shared his new religious experience with Bill Wilson.

When Bill protested that he could not trust the God which formalized religion had presented him in the past, Thacher explained that the Oxford Group encouraged trusting in God—understood not in traditional dogma—but in a growing way, beginning with how the individual understood God to be. (This is the concept which later surfaced in A.A.'s "God *as we understood Him*.") Bill agreed to think this over—in reality, to *drink* it over—but the reunion with Thacher had a profound and lasting impact on him.

The next day, Bill met with another alcoholic, and along with some other acquaintances, went to the Calvary Church Mission on Twenty-Third Street in New York City to explore what Thacher had been talking about. There, Bill heard an enthusiastic presentation of the gospel in a way he never had before. When the invitation was given, he forgot his comrades and pressed his way forward in response. He felt a peace and an exhilaration like nothing he ever had experienced and wanted to shout out his release and happiness. But upon leaving, again facing his drunken companions and others in the streets of Depression-era New York, he convinced himself that what he had experienced was circumstantial emotionalism without lasting importance, and stepped back into the secure, familiar, dark confines of a gin bottle. However, like his initial encounter with Ebby Thacher, this experience would not leave his memory nor depart from his longing.

Bill Wilson had known a longing in his soul ever since he could remember. Friends and relatives back in East Dorset had always said that as a child, Bill would sit alone for long periods of time with arms outstretched, repeating over and over again, "I want . . . I want . . . I want . . . ." Now as the days passed after his conversion at the Calvary Church Mission, Bill's alcoholism worsened. Following a street accident, Dr. Silkworth admitted him to the hospital yet again, sadly certain that this would be the last time. It was there that Bill, tormented by the devastating effects of alcohol toxicity, and viewing himself as wretched, caged and condemned, struggled against what he now knew was certain death. Pleadingly and imploringly, thinking of Ebby Thacher and the Presence and Joy he had experienced at Calvary Church Mission, the little boy from East Dorset once again raised his arms to complete his longing plea for the first time: "I want . . . *to live.*"

Bill would always recall what happened next. He claimed that something like a great, loving light enveloped him. In an echo of his experience at the Mission, he felt physically and mentally at peace, spiritually content and comforted. The wracking agonies of terminal alcoholism left his body, and for the first time in William G. Wilson's empty life of longing, he knew that he was not alone. Satisfaction filled the hunger of his soul.

A surprised Dr. Silkworth called on Wilson the next morning. Instead of the wretched, dying man he expected to encounter, Silkworth was astonished to see a transformed man who could only be described as truly sober and at peace. Although Bill was experiencing some of the same doubts he had known after his conversion at the Mission, Silkworth wisely advised him to hold onto the experience and let it accomplish its work in him. Wilson complied.

When he returned home from the hospital, Wilson had two issues of importance on his mind. One was to immerse himself in Thacher's Oxford Group, using it as a springboard to evangelize other alcoholics. The other was to become productive again, and relieve the financial burden he had placed on his wife.

In his effort to help other alcoholics, Wilson attempted to take them in off the street, house them in his own home and work with them, assisted by Thacher and other sober alcoholics. Initially, this work went badly.

The second concern held more promise. Wilson had not lost his sharp business acumen, and was certain that he could re-establish himself in business. Traveling to Akron, Ohio, he set up a business deal with some prominent businessmen which seemed a sure thing. But his confidence was shattered when, upon learning of his alcoholic past, the businessmen declined to meet with him.

There in the lobby of the Akron, Ohio Mayflower Hotel, Wilson noticed the bar. Trembling, he tried to fight the thoughts which flooded his mind, but the laughter, the clinking of glasses and the piano playing at the bar beckoned him almost hypnotically back to the familiar comfort of alcoholic numbness. Then, almost miraculously, he spied the directory of local churches in the lobby, and after getting a good supply of nickels, went to the public pay phone and began calling clergymen, asking each pastor if he knew of any drunks with whom he could talk. One minister, a Reverend Walter Tunks, was able to comply with Wilson's strange request. A member of his church had met and befriended a Dr. and Mrs. Robert Smith; for some time Dr. Smith had been destroying his medical career due to his compulsive use of alcohol. A short interview was scheduled for 5:00 p.m. the next day. The "short interview" lasted until 11:00 that night!

In that interview, Wilson began to discover what had been missing in his initial outreach to other alcoholics, as well as what he himself needed to keep from ruining his hard-won sobriety: sharing from his own experience, the basis of what later became the twelfth step of A.A. When "Dr. Bob" Smith later became sober, he made the same discovery when he and Wilson met with yet another alcoholic and shared their experiences with him. By the fall of 1935, a small group of sober alcoholics began meeting regularly in Akron.

Despite Wilson's initial zeal for the Oxford Group, he broke with it eventually—in part, because its members disapproved of the alcoholics' emphasis on *their* problem to the neglect of other group concerns. In addition, Wilson felt that in order to reach alcoholics of *all* faiths, religious demands should be played down and tolerance should be played up. Finally, Wilson recognized that part of the power of recovery lay in small groups; the Oxford Group was placing an increasing dependance on larger gatherings.

Wilson and his sober comrades formed the Twelve Steps from the Oxford Groups' emphases on self-examination, restitution, humility, anonymity, simplicity, taking one day at a time and conceptualizing God apart from conventional religious dogma. They also specified the group's purpose through the very first step, which Bill had learned that night in the hospital—acknowledging powerlessness over the addiction, the self-destruction it brings, and seeking God's help and salvation from death.

It is this vague spirituality that many Christians today shy away from and avoid. This is unnecessary, however, as the Twelve Steps are indeed a valuable and successful tool for people with all kinds of addictions. Christians need only realize that we seek to trust God, not as conventional religious dogma presents Him, or even as we *want* to perceive Him, but rather, *as He has revealed Himself in Christ Jesus.*

It is humility which will enable us to do this—humility we must come to grips with in the first of the Twelve Steps. Bill Wilson spent his lifetime struggling with humility. For example, when A.A. was safely and well-established, and Wilson had appeared in national magazines and had gained fame as "America's Number-One Drunk," he ran into an old friend whom he had not seen in years one day at a busy airport. After much hand-pumping and back-slapping, the friend noted that Wilson looked much better than he had remembered him from years ago, and asked what he had been doing with himself during all that time. Exasperated that this man obviously was unaware of his fame, Wilson sputtered, attempting tact, "Well, you know— A.A.!" The friend smiled broadly, declaring that of all the people he knew who needed A.A., Wilson had been the one who needed it most; he sure was glad that Wilson had found help with those people!

Like Bill Wilson, many Christians may need to exercise some humility to explore the Twelve Steps for the universal truths they contain—truths that the Christian Oxford Group knew (but rejected in pridefully expunging "Bill and his drunks" from their fellowship)—realizing that these truths are valuable tools for gaining freedom from *all* addictions.

When we experience the despair of being powerless over our compulsions, we can, like Bill Wilson, begin our new lives by reaching out to God *as He has revealed Himself in Jesus Christ,* and by submitting ourselves to His guidance as He helps us apply universal principles of recovery to our daily lives.

---

* The authors are grateful for biographical information about Bill Wilson found in the book, *Bill W., Fiftieth Anniversary Edition* by Robert Thomsen, (New York: Harper Colophon Books, 1975), and for information about the Oxford Group from "A Short History of Alcoholics Anonymous," by Larry Hart, *Mission Journal,* Feb., 1987, pp. 8-9, 18.

Step One
My Will Is a Won't

We admit that by ourselves we are powerless over our eating behavior—that our lives have become unmanageable.

For I know that nothing good dwells in me, that is, in my flesh; for the wishing is present in me, but the doing of the good is not.
                                                                    Rom. 7:18

Eating disorders wear many faces; they have no respect for a person's age, race, sex, social standing, profession or religious beliefs. Some people seem to be genetically predisposed to eating disorders; others may abuse food for a number of years before crossing the line to addictive food behavior.

Either way, the distinguishing mark of addiction is *powerlessness*. Initially, this may be difficult to grasp because the affect triggered by addictive eating behavior is usually—with prolonged use—one of control. We think we are in control when we are binging or purging or starving. We are apt to feel out of control only when our drug of choice—our food or eating behavior—has been taken away and our comfort level begins to plummet. In reality, any sense of control we gain from our eating-disordered behavior is a misperception, for we find that the more we try to control it, the more out-of-control and unmanageable our lives become.

There usually are two types of people with eating disorders: those who know they are powerless over their dependency but cannot stop, and those who cannot yet see their powerlessness over their binging and purging, eating or starving.

One reason for the inability to recognize signs of powerlessness over a food-related compulsion is the emotional release made possible by addictive food behavior. For example, moving our jaws during an eating binge discharges aggression without our having to face our reasons for being angry—literally, the anger is eaten, the rage is choked and stuffed down. Obsessing about ideal weight, counting calories and exercising compulsively are great activities for making us "feel good" about our lives while avoiding the stress associated with solving complicated problems and relationships.

Purging discharges anger that has been stuffed down so that we can maintain the appearance of "being nice." In reality, failing to solve our primary problems contributes heavily to our powerlessness, making our lives unmanageable.

By the time he becomes involved in treatment (if he is that fortunate), the eating-disordered person usually knows he is hurting, and may want help. But usually he is not willing to recognize his dependency as the culprit for his unhappy situation. Instead, he blames himself, his family, his traumatic or tragic circumstances, his boss, pastor or God. When in treatment, he secretly may hope to resolve these issues in order to return to the eating-disordered behavior (although he would of course deny this is so).

If you suspect that you have an eating-related disorder, it will be necessary for you to examine your life for indications of an addictive food behavior (anorexia nervosa, bulimia nervosa, compulsive eating) and especially, to look for the signs of powerlessness and mismanagement which result from an addictive disorder. Moving forward usually is preceded by looking backward; before we can adequately deal with the present, we must examine our past.

Let's begin by answering the following questions as honestly and as accurately as possible. Put a check mark beside each question that describes your situation.

Anorexia Nervosa

❏ (For women) Do you have irregular periods, or have you experienced total loss of menstruation for at least three cycles when it should otherwise have been expected?

❏ Have you been dieting, not because you are overweight (according to standards based on your age, sex and height), but because you desire to be more slim in your appearance?

❏ Do you claim to "feel" fat when others tell you that you obviously are not overweight?

❏ When others tell you that you are not overweight, do you ever feel annoyed or irritated, perceiving that they are trying to control your body, that they are jealous or that they just cannot understand the needs of your life and your body?

❏ Do you often think about food, calories, body weight, nutrition and cooking, to the extent that such thinking distracts you from other important, though unrelated, responsibilities and tasks?

❏ Does physical exercise occupy a disproportionate amount of your time each day?

❏ Do you weigh yourself frequently, even going out of your way in order to get on a set of scales and check your weight one more time during the day?

❏ Do you fast, induce vomiting, use laxatives or diuretics in order to lose weight?

❏ Do you go to the bathroom immediately after meals? Do you get angry or irritated if it is occupied or if you must delay for some other reason?

❏ Do you often hide and hoard food or act out some other type of food-related behavior which you think is sensible, but which you prefer others not know about?

❏ Do you feel nauseated or bloated when you eat as much as or less than others your own age and size at a normal mealtime without prior snacking?

❏ Do you occasionally binge on food and then feel ashamed of yourself and atone for your overeating by subsequently starving yourself totally for a period of time?

Bulimia Nervosa

❏ Are you fearful of being fat, believing that body fat is a "sin"?

❏ Do you try to diet repeatedly, only to sabotage your plans by binging activities for which you feel great shame?

❏ Do you frequently tend to overestimate your needs for food intake for a given meal or snack, especially "oversnacking" when under stress?

❏ Do you hide and hoard private stashes of food for later binging?

❏ Do you binge on high-calorie, sugary, "forbidden" foods, or on "safe" foods, such as salads?

❏ Do you shroud your eating (especially binges) in secrecy, fearing anyone's scrutiny of your eating behavior?

❏ Do you often feel ashamed and/or depressed when you eat?

❏ Do you spend much time thinking about your next binge, planning it (perhaps in detail), when you should be engaged in other tasks and activities?

• Do thoughts about food occupy much of your time?

• Does any interruption of this thinking result in your feeling cross, irritable and angry, all of which you must hide from anyone else's notice?

❏ Do you induce vomiting in order to get rid of "binge food"?

- Do you exercise to work off a binge?
- Do you use laxatives and/or diuretics in ways other than prescribed to eliminate food you have eaten?
- Do you also engage in any of these behaviors especially to discharge feelings of anger or anxiety which may have accompanied the binge?
❑ Do you disappear to the bathroom or to another available, hidden source of plumbing immediately after meals?
- Do you become anxious or angry if it is occupied or if you cannot use it for any other reason?
❑ If you have been living in a college dorm room with a sink or other source of plumbing, have you ever had to make maintenance calls to repair the plumbing system due to your purging?
❑ Do you binge/purge more than three times a week?
❑ Have you been confronted by others about your behavior (and denied all) and then resolved to start keeping more distance from friends or family members to avoid future confrontations about your food behavior?

Compulsive Eating

❑ Are you overweight despite prompting to lose weight by others, including a physician?
❑ Have you repeatedly attempted to diet, only to fail or sabotage your weight loss?
❑ Do you overeat by binging or by "grazing" (snacking constantly), usually while engaging in other activities?
❑ Do you keep private "stashes" of snacks, hoping to ensure that others will not know about or discover them?
❑ Do you make a lot of self-demeaning or insulting jokes about your food consumption or body weight?
❑ Do you go to some trouble to eat alone, in secrecy?
❑ Is food your "friend"?
❑ Do you have urges to eat when you're feeling sad, angry, afraid, anxious or ashamed, or when you are experiencing other unwelcome emotions?
- As you eat at such times, do you ever think, *I deserve this*?
❑ Do you expend much mental energy thinking about food and eating, especially during times when your mind should be focused on the tasks at hand?

❑ Do you ever feel angry (which must be suppressed and denied so that your feelings will not be known) when you are obstructed or interrupted in any way from eating, especially when you are alone?

❑ Does feeling ashamed of your body weight result in renewed eating binges and/or grazing?

• Do you ever fear that you might be crazy because of these self-defeating behaviors?

❑ When you were a child, did, "Have a cookie" mean, "Shut up"? Do you sense this or a similar type of message when you eat now?

If you have established eating-disordered behavior and thinking in your life, then complete the following questions about powerlessness.

Powerlessness

■ What best describes your compulsive eating behavior (binging and/or purging, hoarding food, avoiding meals, skipping meals, exercising, laxative/diuretic misuse/abuse, "grazing," self-starvation)? Circle those that apply.

■ When did you first begin this/these behavior(s), and why?

■ Why do you think you have continued them?

■ If binging/purging relates to your eating behavior...

• How frequently do you binge? _____ times daily _____ times weekly.

• How frequently do you purge? _____ times daily _____ times weekly.

■ In what amounts do you generally consume food?

■ Do you think your answers to the above questions indicate "normal" eating habits, i.e., like most other people?

■ Have you ever been frightened because you've passed out or coughed up blood when purging?

■ Have you tried to control your food consumption, purging or other eating behavior(s)? _____ If so, how?

• Were you successful for a time? _____ How long at best?

• Did you ultimately fail? _____ If so, why?

■ How has your food behavior been embarrassing, inconvenient or destructive to you and/or others?

■ Estimate how often you think about eating, weight, calories:

■ Do you think that you've lost self-respect as a result of your secret eating compulsion? If so, how?

■ What is it about your behavior that others seem to object to most?

■ How has *powerlessness* over your eating behavior become evident to you?

Unmanageability

■ What does *unmanageability* mean to you?

■ What is your current physical condition (i.e., status of tooth enamel; ability to evacuate your bowels without using laxatives; ability to vomit without several tries or chemical assistance; sensory abilities, especially your sense of hearing and sense of touch; status of menses [monthly periods]; general lethargy and energy levels, concentration and memory)?

• Did you have any of the above problems before you began your compulsive eating behavior(s)?

■ What feelings have you tried to alter or ignore by your compulsive eating behavior(s)?

■ Have you experienced any mood swings or weakness because of blood sugar fluctuations?

■ Give five examples of "social" unmanageability on your part as a result of your eating behavior. ("Social unmanageability" refers to occasions and situations in which your eating behavior has taken priority over the necessary functions of a relationship; for example, feeling a need to binge when expecting an important phone call, and then feeling resentment toward the caller, or even taking the phone off of the hook in order to binge, resulting in an inability to cope with the business which the call involved or even a threat to that business relationship.)

■ Name five ways your eating behavior has led you to anti-social behavior (a behavior which compromises your conscience or values, such as lying, shoplifting, etc.).

■ Name five ways your eating behavior has or may have caused you to mismanage and/or jeopardize your education and/or job.

■ What crises have you experienced as a result of your eating behavior?

■ Have you been in treatment for eating disorders before?_____
More than once? _____ How many times have you been in treatment before? _____

■ If you are in treatment now, describe the crisis which prompted you to seek treatment at this time:

■ Would you call your eating behavior an *addiction*?

Stages of Acceptance

Despite the negative symptoms, consequences and complications of addictive food behavior, and the many benefits associated with recovery, many people who suffer from eating disorders experience profound feelings of loss at the onset of recovery. Though these feelings eventually decline in frequency and intensity, they may last from several weeks to several years, depending on the severity of addiction.

One author has identified five stages experienced by those who are terminally ill.[1] Our observations have confirmed that those withdrawing from eating-disordered behaviors usually pass through similar phases at various intervals during the recovery process:

- **Denial:** Most people with an eating disorder are unable or unwilling to admit that they have a problem—to others or themselves—despite obvious signs that their lives are driven by the disorder.

  Gail was a high achiever who had struggled with her body weight and image since high school. She had been able to maintain what she considered the "ideal weight" by limiting her food intake and exercising compulsively. During college, these habits intensified. Because she had been depriving her body of food, she became preoccupied with it, and when under pressure, lost control and resorted to binge-eating. She would then make herself vomit to eliminate the food she had consumed during the binge.

  After graduating from college, she had landed a job as a sales representative for a national pharmaceutical company, and within 15 months, had climbed to the top. The pressure and lack of structure associated with her job caused Gail more problems with her eating-disordered behavior, and then with her job. She began to run late for her appointments. Then she began missing important calls from clients because her time was increasingly absorbed by the binge/purge cycle which now characterized much of her disorder. Over time, she was unable to attend to her clients' needs. Her sales volume fell, gradually at first, and then sharply over the course of five months until finally, she was unable to produce. The company let her go.

  In response, Gail blamed her boss for his lack of understanding. She blamed the company because the job was "too demanding." When she was unable to find work over the next six months due to the all-consuming demands of her disorder, she blamed God, "who's had it out for me since the beginning."

Gail had been confronted several times by friends and family members about her "food problem."

"Problem? What problem? I've just had a rough go of things," she said.

• **Bargaining:** Bargaining usually marks the beginning of the dependent person's recognition of his or her addiction, and is an attempt to postpone quitting. Bargaining can occur with oneself: *I need to kick this, but I'm just too upset right now. What difference is one more little binge going to make? I'll quit later.* Or, it can be a response to others: "Of course I'm still serious about giving this up, and I will—right after this project at work blows over." Or, it can be a plea to God: "God, help me stop—tomorrow."

• **Anger:** When the eating-disordered person can no longer escape the facts pointing to his or her addiction, and/or when he or she finally enters treatment, anger is a normal response. Frequent objects of anger are God, family members or close friends, all of whom—according to the dependent person—contributed to his or her addiction or entry to treatment. A person's anger also may be directed toward the circumstances of needing to enter recovery, and toward him- or herself for perpetuating this perceived tragedy and for feeling helpless to overcome it alone.

• **Grief:** The majority of eating-disordered persons have become experts at avoiding painful emotions. The experience of deep distress, or grief, during recovery is often an unwelcome surprise.

Many of us associate grief with the loss of a loved one, but feelings of grief are a normal response to the loss of anything we might consider important to our well-being.

Compulsive food behavior often provides an immediate payoff: It may calm our nerves; block feelings of pain, failure or disappointment; or give us a sense of courage, power or control. In addition, because the cycle of addiction turns us increasingly inward, compulsive eating or rigid control over food consumption often becomes a primary means of self-nurturing. When this "support" is taken away, it's like losing a good friend. Grieving over such a loss is a normal, healthy aspect of recovery (even though it doesn't feel good), and is done properly when a person gives him- or herself the freedom to feel the loss whenever it comes to mind.

• **Acceptance:** Over time, those who continue in recovery are able to accept their addiction and their need for treatment. Most are gradually able to maintain a life apart from addictive patterns of behavior with a sense of serenity, and eventually, joy.

■ These stages often overlap in actual experience. Which one(s) are you in now? Describe your present feelings:

For Additional Reflection and Application

Note that step 1 of the Twelve-Steps refers to our being *powerless,* not *helpless* or *hopeless.* This is an important differentiation. To acknowledge powerlessness means, *I must seek the power I do not have in myself. I must seek help for doing what I cannot do myself.*

In Matt 5:3, the first of the Beatitudes, Jesus said, *Blessed are the poor in spirit, for theirs is the kingdom of heaven.*

What an interesting statement! The kingdom of heaven—living eternally in glory with God—can be purchased only by acknowledging poverty! Just imagine going to a local bank and purchasing a house by saying, "I'm too poor to buy a house"! Yet this is the idea behind the first Beatitude: *When I acknowledge that I do not have the strength to free myself from the bondage of my compulsive eating behavior, then I can ask for the help I need and obtain the freedom I desperately need.* We will be dealing with this plea for help in the next two steps.

Step 1 also says that our lives have become *unmanageable,* not *uncontrollable.* Control is what we sought through our compulsive eating behavior to begin with: control over our feelings, body weight and size, in order to secure freedom from the controls others have wielded over us. Our lives, however, are not ours for ownership, but stewardship—we are to serve as faithful managers. Step 1 points us toward regaining appropriate management of our lives. It is the doorway to our recovery, which we pursue by working steps 2 through 12.

Again, we must understand that recovery is a process. It does not provide the immediate gratification we have come to associate with our eating disorder. Rather, because it enables us to grow in ever-increasing freedom and health throughout our lives as God shows us the way, recovery eventually leads to a contentment and peace within that is lasting.

Along the way, you may discover that your addiction is a combination of different problems, but you also will have the satisfaction of seeing many of the problems that developed as a result of your eating disorder subside. Again, this will take time. Be patient with yourself. Be patient with those around you who may not be used to your new patterns of behavior. But above all, continue with the process. It really is worth it!

■ Read Ps. 20:2-3; 51:17; 116:1-9; 147:10-11. Why does admitting weakness to God give Him an opportunity to strengthen us?

■ Read Is. 55:8-9; Jer. 9:23-24; Rom. 7:18-20; 2 Cor. 1:9; 3:4-5. Why is it important to place our trust in God, rather than in ourselves?

■ Read 2 Cor. 12:9-10 and Heb. 11:32-34. What comfort and encouragement do you find in being "weak" before God?

■ Read Eph. 3:14-21, and in the space below, write what you need most from God right now, using this passage to guide you.

■ Which of these passages is most helpful to you, and why?

Step Two
My Humbling Admission

***We come to believe that God, through Jesus Christ,
can restore us to sanity.***

*. . . for it is God who is at work in you, both to will
and to work for His good pleasure.*

Phil. 2:13

There is a story about a man who fell from a high cliff, and who, as he was plunging toward his death, saw and grabbed a branch growing out of the cliff and hung on desperately for dear life. He looked up and saw that the place from which he had fallen would be impossible to reach by climbing. The cliff was too steep. He then looked down from a dizzying height and realized that he could never survive the impact of dropping to the ground. As happens to so many people in desperate situations, it was in this position of great danger that this man thought about God for the first time since his childhood. He had rejected all ideas of religion long ago. Now, as the branch began to strain under the burden of his weight, it occurred to him that this would be a good time to pray.

"Is anyone up there?" he shouted upward (after all, isn't "up there" supposed to be where God is?).

Suddenly, a massive, booming voice responded, "YES, IT IS I. THIS IS THE LORD."

With amazement and gratitude, the man shouted, "Please God, if you can help me, I'll do anything You ask!"

"ANYTHING?"

"Yes! Anything You ask!"

"LET GO OF THE BRANCH!"

The man pondered this command, again looking up, then down. Looking up once more, he shouted, "Is anybody else up there?"

When working the Twelve Steps, and especially when moving from step 1 to step 2, most of us who suffer from addictive behaviors would sympathize with the man in this story. Having surveyed the important questions and admitted our powerlessness and mismanagement of life as a result of addiction, our temptation is to quit before getting into any business about God. Our dilemma feels much like being pushed from a tall height—similar to the platform used by a trapeze artist (and seemingly without a net!)—only to be caught by a great Hand and asked, "DO YOU BELIEVE IN GOD?"

We fell from our trapeze platform in step 1; our challenge now is to acknowledge the Hand that is reaching out to save us.

Sanity

Before confronting this issue, it will be important to deal with a word which appears in step 2 which may seem puzzling, or even provocative: *sanity. Webster's New World Dictionary* defines *sanity* as "soundness of judgment."

Remember the general questions about eating disorders in step 1? Consider the following in light of "soundness of judgment":

- Missing more than three periods (without sexual activity) and failing to consult a doctor.
- "Feeling" fat, when others insist that we are not.
- Believing that others are out to control us when they fearfully point out that we look like we just got out of a concentration camp.
- Thinking about food (because we resist eating most of the time) when we should be taking a Physics exam, or engaged in another important task.
- Exercising for a full quarter of the day's time.
- Weighing ourselves ten minutes after the last time we weighed (which was ten minutes after the previous time), as if we breathed ten pounds onto ourselves in that time.
- Taking thirty Correctol to get rid of a cookie.
- Hoarding food like a squirrel hoards nuts, even when we resist eating it.
- Eating a cookie and then starving ourselves for two days to "atone" for our "sin."
- Thinking of a food—a non-conscious, inanimate object—as a "friend" or an "enemy."
- Being afraid of having others see us eat.
- Spending tremendous amounts of money on "junk food," then throwing it up, then shoplifting it when we run out of money and then viewing eating, not stealing, as a sin.
- Making ourselves throw up (which we believe is fine), but hating to get a stomach flu because it makes us throw up.

- Continuing to overeat when our physician says that our health is imperiled by our body weight.
- Riding the diet "roller coaster," losing weight only to regain it, in a cyclical fashion.
- Hiding cookies and candy from others as if these snacks were gold from Fort Knox.
- Waiting anxiously for everyone else in the house to go to bed so that we can make something to eat.
- When feeling *lonely* (which means, *I'm alone—go find company*), we go to the "fridge" instead.
- "Wolfing" down food like a wild animal.
- When noting that we are overweight, feeling ashamed of ourselves and going to a fast-food place to get something to eat.

The Binge/Purge Cycle

Yet another illustration of "insanity" is the cycle of binging and purging which characterizes bulimic behavior. When the bulimic experiences intense emotions, he or she usually copes by engaging in a food binge. The result of such binging is another experience of intense emotions, with which the bulimic attempts to cope through a purge. This, in turn, produces more strong emotions, creating a cycle to which the bulimic rigidly adheres.

The chart on the following page illustrates this cycle.

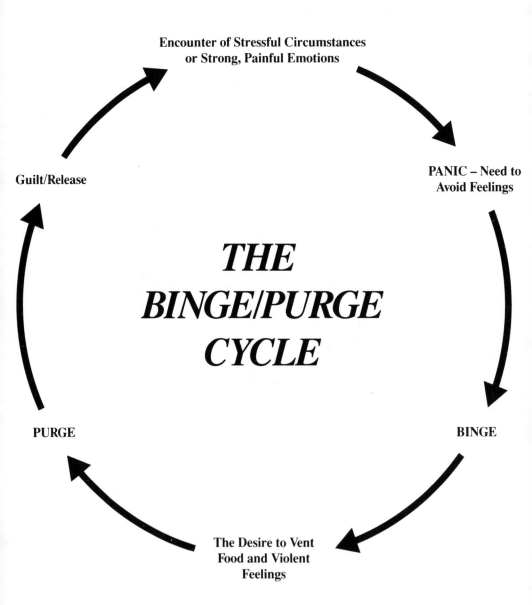

Encounter of Stressful Circumstances
or Strong, Painful Emotions

PANIC – Need to
Avoid Feelings

THE
BINGE/PURGE
CYCLE

Guilt/Release

BINGE

PURGE

The Desire to Vent
Food and Violent
Feelings

In effect, the binge/purge cycle amounts to "barking up the wrong tree." The insanity of this behavior is that it not only is harmful, but fails to address the issues surrounding the intense emotions to begin with. "Sanity," in this case, would mean questioning the reason for one's intense emotions and then dealing with the issues which prompted those emotions; in other words, *solving the problem(s)*. Unless one squarely faces the issues surrounding unwelcome emotions, he or she is likely to continue in the insanity of addiction. This will prevent resolution of the problem by brushing it aside, by "barking up the wrong tree."

If any of the above scenarios illustrate a lack of sound judgment, then we can conclude that the behaviors which characterize eating disorders are insane, and that our "sanity" is a pressing need.

Acknowledging the truth that eating-disordered behavior is insane is like waking up from a fog. In step 2, we seek restored sanity as a gift from God.

• List five occasions when you have acted in such a way that an objective observer, who knows you and your circumstances, might say, "That's insane!" (You may wish to refer to the above list, if any apply to you).

Complications in Our Views of God

If talking about God makes you feel uncomfortable, that is perfectly understandable. You may perceive God as a restrictive, overly-controlling parent-figure, as an all-too-powerful and vengeful righter of wrongs or as some other negative figure of authority. Each of us tends to "make God in our own image," or ascribe to Him those characteristics we've observed in other figures of authority. We may avoid Him by exercising our own "lordship," acting as "fourth persons of the Trinity," rigidly and defensively controlling our lives, fearful of any lapse in our self-sufficiency. We may insist on perfecting ourselves by ourselves, and when we fail to attain to our rigid standards, heap shame upon ourselves. We may blame those whom we view as obstacles to our goals, including those who have hurt us in the past, and who thereby have contributed to our problems. We especially may tend to blame God—perhaps even denying His existence—because He has refused to cooperate with our plans and desires, or because He has not prevented our past painful experiences. And now we are believe that *this* God can restore us to sanity?

No. To do so only would contribute to more of the insanity characteristic of our eating disorder. Notice what step 2 says: *We come to believe that God, through Jesus Christ, can restore us to sanity.*

Once we "come to" from the fog that characterized our eating disorder, (that is, recognize the insanity of our behavior), we begin to realize that we have been wrong about a great many things, including our concepts of God.

In the past, we may have avoided God because of our personal sense of inadequacy, and especially our sense of guilt and shame. These feelings may have prompted us to shy away from Him, fearing that He would condemn and punish us for our failures and shortcomings.

Perhaps you feel guilty about the behaviors you indicated as insane. Or, as in the case with many who are bound by eating disorders, perhaps you were abused in some way as a child, and believing that you somehow were to blame for the abuse, you feel a sense of shame as a result of the abusive interaction. Perhaps your eating disorder, as well as your attempts to hide from God, really are part of your strategy to avoid feelings of guilt and shame.

If any of the above is true of you, it may be helpful to explore an understanding of what *guilt* and *shame* are.

Guilt

For our purposes, we will distinguish between real and false guilt with *guilt* and *perceived guilt*. "Guilt" is a judicial fact, the truth that we have done something that was, in fact, inappropriate and/or wrong. "Perceived guilt" is the perception that we are guilty, even though we may not actually have done anything wrong.

Sue was mad at Cliff because he had revealed something to a friend which she'd told him in confidence. Finally, when she could bear her anger no longer, she confronted him with his wrongdoing and her subsequent anger in an appropriate way.

Now Sue has the uneasy feeling of perceived guilt. She is not really guilty of any wrongdoing, but because she confronted Cliff, and especially because she was raised to believe, *If you can't say anything nice, don't say anything at all,* she *perceives* guilt on her part.

Dale is in trouble. His neighbor has two small children, and each seems able to generate the aggravation of ten children with their boisterous behavior and noise. They threw a baseball through one of Dale's new storm windows, which bounced off the wall and came out and broke another window. Dale picked up the ball, and in his anger, threw it at one of the children. The ball hit the child in the head. The children didn't see Dale and no one seems to know who hit the child with the baseball. Now Dale feels guilty, and rightly so. He actually is guilty of vengefully hurting his neighbor's child.

Sally and Mark seem like the perfect couple. They communicate well, have many mutual interests and obviously enjoy each other's company. They are head-over-heels in love with each other, which is unfortunate since both are married to someone else. They have been sexually intimate with one another a number of times, but feel no remorse for this because they are so in love with each other. They neglect their spouses and their children because they are so in love with each other. They feel no guilt because they are so in love with each other. But they really are guilty of adultery, whether they *feel* guilty or not.

Shame

Shame generally results from the experience of feeling or being exposed and failing to measure up, either in one's own estimation or in that of another. Resulting feelings of inadequacy and hopelessness often result in conjunction with feelings of real or perceived guilt because of one's own or another's wrongdoing.

Margaret was sexually abused by her father throughout her adolescence. These experiences at once horrified and shocked her and gave her pleasure. On the one hand, she enjoyed being her father's "special girl," his "little princess," and of course, she could not help her physical responses to his touch (although she sometimes wondered if this were, in fact, true). On the other hand, she felt disgusted and violated by his behavior, frightened by the prospect that he might harm her or reject her if she failed to comply, and fearful of what others might say or do if only they knew.

As Margaret grew into adulthood, she longed for intimacy in her relationships with men, and attempted to find it in the only way she knew how—through sexual activity. Although she seemed confident and sure, Margaret felt inadequate in almost every respect outside of the bedroom. She felt that she had nothing to offer or contribute to life but her body. That she allowed men to use her later caused her to be contemptuous toward all men in general. But her primary target of hatred was herself, a hatred that was manifested by her self-deprecating jokes, her compulsive use of alcohol and tobacco, her tendency to be perfectionistic and her self-sacrificing workaholism.

When Margaret became a Christian and began working through her sexual-abuse issues in her late forties, she eventually realized that in addition to the shame she felt for her promiscuity (which was legitimate), she was deeply ashamed of her behavior with her father. She had internalized a deep, heart-felt conviction that she had led him on (thus, she perceived the initial abuse as her fault) and that she could have done more than protest to make him stop the behavior (she believed that the continued abuse also was her fault). Helping Margaret understand that she was not to blame for her father's abusive behavior marked the beginning of her freedom from falsely-based shame.

■ How would you describe feelings of guilt?

■ When you perceive guilt and feel accompanying shame, do you turn to eating-disordered behaviors to push those feelings away? Explain:

■ How have guilt/shame affected . . .
   • your self-esteem?

   • your relationship with your family?

   • your relationships with others?

   • your relationship with God?

Blame
   Still another obstacle to an intimate relationship with God is blame. As our eating disorders progressed, we spent increasing amounts of mental and emotional energy on acquiring or refusing food, exercising control, maintaining or improving body appearance and weight. We became totally

self-absorbed and would have completely lost touch with others were it not for our attempts to manipulate their approval. The low self-esteem which is fed by such thinking and behavior readily lends itself to blame—of others and/or ourselves—for problems, difficulties, disappointments, failures and hurts. "Find a scapegoat!" says blame, looking for a way to escape pain and going for the most accessible target. The problem is, whether we blame others or ourselves, blame cannot change our situation. It cannot reverse our circumstances; it cannot correct anything. It is an exercise in futility! Blame promises power to right a wrong, but cannot deliver on its promise.

We need to discover what role blame has played in our eating disorders and in sabotaging our relationships with God.

■ How do you feel when you fail?

• How do you usually respond to your failures?

■ How do you feel when others fail?

• How do you respond to others when they fail?

■ List the various ways we condemn others or ourselves (i.e., punishment and retaliation through verbal/nonverbal, observable/non-observable means):

■ Which of these do you tend to use? Explain:

• How do you feel when you engage in these behaviors?

• How do others feel/respond when you engage in these behaviors?

■ Do you blame God? If so, describe how and why:

■ Do you believe God has a condemning attitude toward you? If so, describe how and why:

Come to Believe...

This is tough, isn't it? Many of us have wanted to please God, but after repeated failure, have believed ourselves incapable of gaining His approval. Many of us have concluded that we just don't have enough faith, and have consequently despaired of ever having His love and acceptance. In short, we have exerted ourselves to the best of our people-pleasing abilities, thinking that "just a little more" would be the ticket, convinced that "more faith" was something we could generate through our usual control mechanisms.

Happily, we are told differently in the Bible. Consider the following:

> *For it is by grace you have been saved, through faith—*
> *and this not from yourselves, it is the gift of God—not by*
> *works, so that no one can boast.*
> *For we are God's workmanship, created in Christ*
> *Jesus to do good works, which God prepared in advance*
> *for us to do.*
>
> Eph. 2:8-10, NIV

■ Paraphrase the above passage:

• What does this passage say about the origin of faith?

• What does it mean to be "God's workmanship"?

> *And without faith it is impossible to please God,*
> *because anyone who comes to him must believe that he*
> *exists, and that he rewards those who earnestly seek him.*
>
> Heb. 11:6, NIV

■ Paraphrase the above passage:

22

■ What might be the "reward" to which this verse refers?

Whether or not you believe any of the obstacles we've mentioned are true of you, if you are feeling distant from God, know that no one plans to force Him on you. Rather, our intent is to present you with an opportunity to examine your current perceptions of Him and correct any that you may find faulty.

Your Parents and You

Our views of God, our self-concepts and our abilities to relate to others are primarily shaped by our parental relationships. If our parents were loving and supportive, we probably believe that God is loving and strong. If, however, our parents were harsh and demanding, we may believe that God is impossible to please. Either way, the foundation of our emotional, relational and spiritual health usually is established by parental modeling, and the results can be wonderful or tragic.[1]

In order to gain a better understanding of this "shaping" process, it is helpful to examine characteristics of our parents and our relationships with them.

The following is an exercise to help you evaluate your relationship with your father as you were growing up.[2] Check the appropriate squares as you recall how he related to you when you were young. Here is an example:

Characteristics	Always	Very often	Some-times	Hardly Ever	Never	Don't Know
Gentle			✔			
Stern	✔					
Loving			✔			
Aloof			✔			
Disapproving		✔				

WHEN I WAS A CHILD, MY FATHER WAS...

Characteristics	Always	Very often	Some-times	Hardly Ever	Never	Don't Know
Gentle						
Stern						
Loving						
Aloof						
Disapproving						
Distant						
Close and Intimate						
Kind						
Angry						
Caring						
Demanding						
Interested						
Disciplinal						
Gracious						
Harsh						
Wise						
Holy						
Leader						
Provident						
Trustworthy						
Joyful						
Forgiving						
Good						
Cherishing of Me						
Compassionate						
Impatient						
Unreasonable						
Strong						
Protective						
Passive						
Encouraging						
Sensitive						
Just						
Unpredictable						

Evaluation of Your Relationship with Your Father
■ What does this inventory tell you about your relationship with your father?

■ If you were an objective observer of the type of relationship you have just described, how would you feel about the father?

■ About the child?

■ How would you respond to the father? Be specific.

■ To the child?

Now complete thesame exercise, this time to evaluate your relationship with your mother:[3]

WHEN I WAS A CHILD, MY MOTHER WAS...

Characteristics	Always	Very often	Some-times	Hardly Ever	Never	Don't Know
Gentle						
Stern						
Loving						
Aloof						
Disapproving						
Distant						
Close and Intimate						
Kind						
Angry						
Caring						
Demanding						
Interested						
Disciplinal						
Gracious						
Harsh						
Wise						
Holy						
Leader						
Provident						
Trustworthy						
Joyful						
Forgiving						
Good						
Cherishing of Me						
Compassionate						
Impatient						
Unreasonable						
Strong						
Protective						
Passive						
Encouraging						
Sensitive						
Just						
Unpredictable						

Evaluation of Your Relationship with Your Mother

■ What does this inventory tell you about your relationship with your mother?

■ If you were an objective observer of the type of relationship you have just described, how would you feel about the mother?

■ About the child?

■ How would you respond to the mother? Be specific.

■ To the child?

Evaluating Your Relationship with God

We can begin to see how our relationships with our parents have influenced our perceptions of God when we evaluate our present relationship with Him. The following inventory will help you to determine some of your feelings toward God.[4] Because it is subjective, there are no right or wrong answers. To ensure that the test reveals your actual feelings, please follow the instructions carefully.

- Answer openly and honestly. Don't respond from a theological knowledge of God, but from personal experience.

- Don't describe what the relationship ought to be, or what you hope it will be, but what it is right now.

- Some people feel God might be displeased if they give a negative answer. Nothing is further from the truth. He is pleased with our honesty. A foundation of transparency is required for growth to occur.

- Turn each characteristic into a question. For example: *To what degree do I really feel that God loves me? To what degree do I really feel that God understands me?*

TO WHAT DEGREE DO I REALLY FEEL GOD IS...

Characteristics	Always	Very often	Some-times	Hardly Ever	Never	Don't Know
Gentle						
Stern						
Loving						
Aloof						
Disapproving						
Distant						
Close and Intimate						
Kind						
Angry						
Caring						
Demanding						
Interested						
Disciplinal						
Gracious						
Harsh						
Wise						
Holy						
Leader						
Provident						
Trustworthy						
Joyful						
Forgiving						
Good						
Cherishing of Me						
Compassionate						
Impatient						
Unreasonable						
Strong						
Protective						
Passive						
Encouraging						
Sensitive						
Just						
Unpredictable						

■ What does this exercise tell you about your relationship with God?

■ Are there any differences between what you know (theologically) and how you feel (emotionally) about Him? If so, what are they?

Your Father's Influence on Your Relationship with God

Now that we have examined your current relationship with God, let's look at how your relationship with your earthly father has influenced your perception of your heavenly Father.[5]

To make a comparison, transfer all of the check marks you made for your own father on page 24 to the *shaded columns* on page 31. When you have completed this, transfer the check marks you made on page 29 which relate to your relationship with God. To make them more obvious, use an "✗" for this category. Put them in the *white columns* in the appropriate places.

Characteristics	Always	Very often	Some-times	Hardly Ever	Never	Don't Know
Gentle		✗	✔			
Stern	✔	✗				
Loving		✗	✔			
Aloof		✔		✗		
Disapproving			✔			

Instructions: Transfer all check marks from page 24 to the SHADED columns. Transfer all check marks from page 29 to the WHITE columns.

Characteristics	Always	Very often	Some-times	Hardly Ever	Never	Don't Know
Gentle						
Stern						
Loving						
Aloof						
Disapproving						
Distant						
Close and Intimate						
Kind						
Angry						
Caring						
Demanding						
Interested						
Disciplinal						
Gracious						
Harsh						
Wise						
Holy						
Leader						
Provident						
Trustworthy						
Joyful						
Forgiving						
Good						
Cherishing of Me						
Compassionate						
Impatient						
Unreasonable						
Strong						
Protective						
Passive						
Encouraging						
Sensitive						
Just						
Unpredictable						

■ Which characteristics are the same for both your father and your heavenly Father?

■ Which characteristics are quite different (two or more boxes away from each other)?

■ What patterns (if any) do you see?

■ Write a summary paragraph about how your perception of God has been shaped by your relationship with your father:

Your Mother's Influence on Your Relationship with God

How has your mother influenced your perception of your heavenly Father?[6] To get a comparison, transfer all the check marks you made for your mother on page 26 to the *shaded columns* on page 34. Use a check mark for this category.

When you have completed this, transfer the check marks you made on page 29, which relate to your relationship with God. To make them more obvious, use an "✗" for this category. Put them in the *white columns* in the appropriate places.

Characteristics	Always	Very often	Some- times	Hardly Ever	Never	Don't Know
Gentle		✗	✔			
Stern	✔	✗				
Loving		✗	✔			
Aloof		✔		✗		
Disapproving			✔			

Instructions: Transfer all check marks from page 26 to the SHADED columns. Transfer all check marks from page 29 to the WHITE columns.

Characteristics	Always	Very often	Some-times	Hardly Ever	Never	Don't Know
Gentle						
Stern						
Loving						
Aloof						
Disapproving						
Distant						
Close and Intimate						
Kind						
Angry						
Caring						
Demanding						
Interested						
Disciplinal						
Gracious						
Harsh						
Wise						
Holy						
Leader						
Provident						
Trustworthy						
Joyful						
Forgiving						
Good						
Cherishing of Me						
Compassionate						
Impatient						
Unreasonable						
Strong						
Protective						
Passive						
Encouraging						
Sensitive						
Just						
Unpredictable						

■ Which characteristics are the same for both your mother and your heavenly Father?

■ Which characteristics are quite different (two or more boxes away from each other)?

■ What patterns (if any) do you see?

■ Write a summary paragraph about how your perception of God has been shaped by your relationship with your mother:

Learning More About God from Psalm 139

Some passages in Scripture highlight certain aspects of our relationship with God. Psalm 139 is a perfect example of this because it describes God's character in a number of ways. Studying this psalm can help you understand how His *omniscience* (being all-knowing), *omnipresence* (being ever-present) and *omnipotence* (being all-powerful) can apply to you and your circumstances.

We will examine a few verses from this psalm at a time. Then we will ask questions to promote reflection.[7]

God Knows Me Thoroughly
■ Read verses 1-4.
- God always knows everything about you. You can keep no secrets from Him, yet He loves you unconditionally! How does this make you feel?

- In what ways does God's omniscience give you courage and strength?

He Protects Me
■ Read verses 5-6.
- God's perfect knowledge about you enables Him to protect you (to hem you in). From what do you need His protection?

- Is it difficult for you to understand the Lord's omniscience? Why or why not?

He Is Always Present
■ Read verses 7-12.
- The most important assurance to one who has strayed is that he is not lost! How close is God to you?

- How close does He seem to be?

- How far can you get from Him?

He Is a Sovereign Creator
■ Read verses 13-15.
- Who is responsible for the creation of your body?

- Do you believe that the One who created you can also restore you? Why, or why not?

- Can you rejoice that you look exactly the way the Father wants you to look? Why, or why not?

- How do you normally respond to your appearance?

- How does your perception of your appearance affect your self-image?

- Do you think (or worry) about what other people think of your appearance? Why or why not?

• How could this psalm help free you from the fear of what others think of you?

God Has a Plan for You
■ Read verse 16.
• Describe any comfort you gain from knowing that God has a plan for your life:

• What types of plans do you suppose God might have for you? Examples:

He wants me to have a relationship with Him through His Son, Jesus Christ (John 3:16-18).
He wants to provide for my welfare, and give me a future and a hope (Jer. 29:11).
He wants to give me things that will be good for me (Matt. 7:7-11).
He wants to strengthen me (Is. 40:29).
He wants me to spend eternity with Him (John 14:1-3).

God Is Constant and Consistent
■ Read verses 17-18.
• The Lord is infinite and He is thinking about you all the time! How does that fact comfort and encourage you?

Our Response

■ Read verses 23-24.

Openness to God's correction and guidance is the way the psalmist responds to the secure position he has with God. You also can have a secure position with God, through Jesus Christ, who died to pay for your sins and rose from the dead to give you new life.

• Are you open to God's correction and guidance? Why or why not?

Sponsorship

Being open to God's correction and guidance often involves considering input and feedback from those who have developed some maturity, both in their relationship with God and in a life apart from compulsive-addictive behavior. A mature sponsor can be a tremendous asset to our recovery. Preferably this person is someone who also is in recovery for eating disorders, who is working through a twelve-step format like ours, but who has a minimum of one year's time (preferably more) in recovery, and who can supervise our "step work" and be available to us in emergencies. A trusted friend or clergyman will do, although our best bet is with a sponsor in recovery or a Christian counselor who specializes in eating disorders.

A sponsor should be someone who has maturity and wisdom regarding recovery issues, and who is willing to establish appropriate boundaries with us. This means having an ability to give help without trying to "save" us when what is best for our growth and development is responsibly facing problems, making choices and living with the consequences. The good sponsor teaches and helps, but leaves us free to make our own decisions.

For Additional Reflection and Application

■ Read Matt. 9:12-13.
• What comfort does this passage give you?

- Do you believe that God, through Jesus Christ, can restore you to "sanity"?

■ Read Mark 9:23-24.
- If you do not believe that God can restore you to "sanity," how can you follow the father's example in this passage?

- Are you willing to ask God to help you in your unbelief?

Belief Systems

By completing this step, you are on your way to becoming familiar with both your perception of God and what Scripture tells us about His ways. Understanding the truth of God's Word is the beginning of our restoration. Throughout the four gospels, Jesus repeatedly emphasized the importance of believing Him. Why? Because our actions usually are based on what we believe!

The book, *The Search for Significance* (McGee), identifies four false beliefs which distort our perceptions of God and ourselves. All of these lies are based on the primary belief that our **self-worth = performance + others' opinions.** In other words, we suffer from a misconception that our significance, or worth, is determined by what we do and what others think of us. Each of these four false beliefs results in a specific fear:

False Belief: *I must meet certain standards to feel good about myself. If I fail to meet these standards, I cannot really feel good about myself.* This belief results in the **fear of failure.**

False Belief: *I must be approved* (accepted) *by certain people to accept myself. If I do not have the approval of these people, I cannot accept myself.* This belief results in the **fear of rejection.**

False Belief: *Those who fail are unworthy of love and deserve to be blamed and condemned.* This belief leads to the **fear of punishment and the propensity to punish others.**

False Belief: *I am what I am. I cannot change. I am hopeless. This means I am simply a total of all my past performances, both good and bad. I am what I have done.* This belief leads to a **sense of shame.**

Each of these false beliefs has a corresponding truth from God's Word, the Scriptures:

SATAN'S LIE:	GOD'S TRUTH:
Your Worth = Your Performance Plus Others' Opinions.	Your Worth = What God Says About You.
Those who fail are unworthy of love and deserve to be blamed and condemned. (Fear of punishment; propensity to punish others).	Propitiation (1 John 4:9-10): *I am deeply loved by God.*
I must meet certain standards to feel good about myself. If I don't...(Fear of failure).	Justification (Rom. 3:19-25; 2 Cor. 5:21): *I am completely forgiven and fully pleasing to God.*
I must be approved (accepted) by certain others to feel good about myself. If I'm not approved...(Fear of rejection).	Reconciliation (Col. 1:19-22): *I am totally accepted by God.*
I am what I am; I cannot change; I am hopeless. (Shame).	Regeneration (2 Cor. 5:17): *I am absolutely complete in Christ.*

Renewing our perception of God, others and ourselves by changing our belief systems will take time, study and experience. It has taken years to develop patterns of behavior that reflect a false belief system. It will take time to change. We will continue to examine these beliefs throughout this workbook. The process of learning to apply God's truth to our lives may be painful at times, but it also is rich, rewarding and exciting!

Summary

Step 2 deals with our believing in God and our restoration to sanity; in fact, in tying the two together, we must conclude that sanity and believing go hand-in-hand. In this step, *believing* involves an acknowledgment that He really exists, that none of us is God and that we may have some misperceptions about God as a result of negative past experiences with other figures of authority. But believing involves more than giving assent to theological doctrine and acquiring knowledge. Step 2 is a tool for examining our overall belief systems. We are now ready for step 3, in which we will deal with another aspect of our believing. It is, in fact, the most important aspect of faith, and would have saved the poor man hanging onto the branch of that cliff.

Relapse

Before moving to step 3, it is important to learn something about relapse. Relapse is returning to an addictive behavior (such as an eating disorder) after a period of abstinence. Relapse is a possibility for anyone in recovery, regardless of how long he or she has abstained from a particular behavior. It is therefore important to be alert to signs pointing toward relapse.

■ Warning Signals

Relapse is a process comprised of behaviors, attitudes, feelings and thoughts which culminate in eating-disordered activity. One may fall into a relapse over a period of hours, days, weeks or even months. Warning signals to alert you to a possible relapse are:

- Feeling uneasy, afraid and anxious, sometimes about abstaining from the addictive behavior. This begins to increase as "serenity" decreases.
- Ignoring feelings of fear and anxiety, and refusing to talk about them with others.
- Having a low tolerance for frustration.
- Becoming defiant, so that rebelliousness begins to replace what has been love and acceptance. Anger becomes one's ruling emotion.
- The "ISM" (I-self-me) attitude grows. Self-centered behavior begins to rule one's attitudes and feelings.
- Increasing dishonesty, whereby small lies begin to surface as deceptive thinking again takes over.
- Increased isolation and withdrawal characterized by missing groups and withdrawing from friends, family and other support.
- Exhibiting a critical, judgmental attitude, a behavior which often is a process of projection as the person in recovery feels shame and guilt for his or her negative behaviors.
- Overconfidence manifested by statements such as, "I'll never do that again," or by simply believing that one is the "exception" to all rules about recovery.
- Lack of confidence about oneself manifested by self-derogatory remarks, overwhelming feelings of failure, a tendency to set oneself up for failure.

■ Special Stressors

In addition to these warning signals, it is important to be alert to certain times which can make one more vulnerable to relapse. Some of these include:

- Completing the first week of abstinence.
- Completing the first twenty-one days of abstinence, and any anniversaries thereafter, specifically: ninety days, six months, nine months, one year.
- Holidays.
- Personal anniversaries, birthdays or other special days.
- Experiencing "high" moods of exuberance, perhaps after receiving a raise, getting a job, getting engaged or married, etc. (Many people fail to realize that "high" moods are as stressful as low moods.)
- Becoming overly hungry, angry, lonely or tired. Using the acronym, HALT (Hungry, Angry, Lonely, Tired) can be helpful in avoiding a potential relapse.

"Triggers" to compulsive behavior often can be defeated by recognizing them and by planning ahead. Step 10 explores a specific strategy we can use to prevent relapse. Feel free to turn to that step now if you foresee needing help with this issue.

Should you relapse and begin the cycle of your eating disorder again, do not let feelings of failure or guilt or a sense of "blowing it" dominate your actions so that you "give in" to the behavior in increasing amounts. Talk to your sponsor, counselor, physician or pastor. (Secrecy only perpetuates addictive behavior.) Look at a "slip" as a deviation from your plan, and then resume your plan for recovery at once.

Step Three
My Saving Decision

We make a decision to turn our lives over to God through Jesus Christ.

I urge you therefore, brethren, by the mercies of God, to present your bodies a living and holy sacrifice, acceptable to God, which is your spiritual service of worship.

Rom. 12:1

You are in a boat on a rough sea. You grip as tightly to the rails as you can to maintain your balance and keep from falling overboard, but a wave comes along which is decidedly more powerful than your grip. You are washed overboard, and upon landing in the water, suddenly recall that you cannot swim (step 1). You become aware that others are still in the boat, and that they have a life preserver. You call to them for help (step 2), and they throw the life preserver in the water, right in front of you. You believe that it can save you from drowning. Now what?

Now you are ready for the second all-important part of believing. You need to trust the life preserver by choosing to put your life in its care.

However, once you have chosen to put on the life preserver, you must choose to continue wearing it until you are safely on board again. If you instead choose to remove it, you will return to your previous predicament—drowning in the overpowering sea, powerless against its forcefulness. Your safety will be assured only if you continuously choose to remain within the safe confines of the life preserver, not if you choose to rely on your own swimming ability.

Step 3 bears similar meaning. Believing in God by intellectual assent is not enough. We need to add trust to make our belief complete, realizing that such trust is a continuous act, not just a one-time event.

Deliverance Comes from God

It is important to understand a basic principle: God respects you! This may seem an odd concept, but it is true. Respect can be measured by the amount of freedom we're given to make personal choices and decisions. God has made us in His Image, and as such, has given us the ability to make choices. Scripture is full of references to God's *chosen* ones (see, for example, Is. 41:9; 42:1; 43:10, 20; 44:1; 65:9; John 13:18; Acts 1:2; 10:41; Col. 3:12; Rev. 17:14, NASB). In like manner, God has throughout the ages extended the privilege and responsibility of making choices to His people. He extended this freedom to Adam and Eve, allowing them to *choose* between long-term fulfillment based on a relationship with Him and short-term fulfillment based on their fleshly desires. They *chose* rebellion against Him, just as their son, Cain, *chose* envy and murder in his relationship with Abel. When Jesus approached the invalid at the pool of Bethesda, He asked, "Do you *want* to be healed?" (John 5:6). In this context, the invalid had to *choose* to take responsibility for himself by getting up and leaving a place of dependency on others.

Choices always involve us in responsibility. In recovery, we learn that irresponsible choices are, in part, the source of an addiction like an eating disorder; responsible choices are part of the solution.

Deliverance from an eating disorder—restoration to physical, emotional, mental and spiritual wholeness—and reconciliation to God only are possible when we place our trust in God's Son, Jesus Christ.

Placing our trust in Christ alone for our salvation is a one-time event through which we are forever saved from our sins and brought into an eternal relationship with God. However, living in submission to Him is a daily (sometimes hourly!) choice. Probably few of us relish the concept of being submissive in any kind of relationship, but Scripture says we will become slaves of that which we obey (Rom. 6:16). In the case of our eating disorder, we have a choice: to submit to our compulsion and allow it to direct our lives as before, or to submit to God and allow Him to be a source of new direction for us.

God knows that we will only follow one whom we know and trust (John 10:3-5). Our purpose in writing this step is to help you build upon your knowledge of God and understand why He is trustworthy. At the same time, we also want to equip you with an understanding of why man has a tendency to refuse God's help and trust instead in himself.

The Fall of Man
The Old Testament depicts the original incident of sin and the Fall of Man:

When the woman saw that the tree was good for food,
and that it was a delight to the eyes, and that the tree was
desirable to make one wise, she took from its fruit and ate;
and she gave also to her husband with her, and he ate.

Then the eyes of both of them were opened, and they
knew that they were naked; and they sewed fig leaves
together and made themselves loin coverings.

Gen. 3:6-7

To understand the devastating effects of this event properly, we need to examine the nature of man prior to sin. Adam, the first created man, was complete and perfectly made in the image of God (Gen. 1:27). His purpose was to reflect God's glory by demonstrating His holiness (Ps. 99:3-5), love and patience (1 Cor. 13:4), forbearance (1 Cor. 13:7), wisdom (James 3:13, 17), comfort (2 Cor. 1:3-4), forgiveness (Heb. 10:17), faithfulness (Ps. 89:1, 2, 5, 8) and grace (Ps. 111:4).

Adam was God's most important creation. To meet his needs for companionship and understanding, God created a woman for Adam and gave her to him as his wife. So great was His approval of this couple that He blessed them so that they could bear children, and commanded them to *fill the earth, and subdue it; and rule over the fish of the sea and over the birds of the sky, and over every living thing that moves on the earth* (Gen. 1:28).

Then God planted a garden in an area called Eden, which means "delight," and which was surrounded by an abundance of resources (see Gen. 2:8-14). Here, God placed Adam and his wife to cultivate the garden and keep it (Gen. 2:15). To satisfy their spiritual needs, God visited Adam and Eve and talked with them personally.

Adam and Eve were perfect in body, mind and spirit, and were free to enjoy all that was within their perfect environment, with one exception:

And the Lord God commanded the man, saying, "From
any tree of the garden you may eat freely;
"but from the tree of the knowledge of good and evil
you shall not eat, for in the day that you eat from it you shall
surely die."

Gen. 2:16-17

Like Adam and Eve, Satan also was created in perfection. At the time of his creation, his name was Lucifer, which means "morning star." He was an angel of the highest rank, created to glorify God. Sadly, Lucifer's pride caused him to rebel against God, and he was cast from heaven with a third of the angels (Is. 14:12-15). When he appeared to Adam and Eve in the garden, it was in the form of a serpent, *more crafty than any beast of the field which the Lord God had made* (Gen. 3:1).

Although Adam had been given authority over the earth, if he rebelled against God as Lucifer had done, he would lose his authority and perfection. He would become a slave to Satan and to sin, and would be a child of God's wrath (Rom. 6:17; Eph. 2:3). Therefore, destroying man was Satan's attempt to reign over the earth and to thwart God's glorious plan for man.

To accomplish this goal, Satan deceived Eve, who fell to the temptation. Eve ate of the tree of the knowledge of good and evil, believing it would make her wise and like God. Adam, however, was not deceived. He deliberately chose to forsake the love and security of God and follow Eve in sin. Paul explained this fact to Timothy:

> *And it was not Adam who was deceived, but the woman being quite deceived, fell into transgression.*
>
> 1 Tim. 2:14

As a result of Adam's decision, he lost the glory God had intended for mankind and forfeited his close fellowship with God. Adam's deliberate rebellion also aided Satan's purpose, giving him power and authority on earth. From that moment on, all history led to a single hill outside of Jerusalem, where God appointed a Savior to pay the penalty for man's sin of rebellion.

Though we justly deserve God's wrath because of that deliberate rebellion (our attempts to find security and purpose apart from Him), His Son became our substitute, experienced the wrath our rebellion deserves and paid the penalty for our sins. Christ's death is the most overwhelming evidence of God's love for us. Because Christ paid for our sins, our relationship with God has been restored, and we are able to partake of His nature and character, to commune with Him and to reflect His love to all the world.

Let's look at some of the characteristics of Christ that we begin to experience when we place our trust in Him.

Characteristics of Christ

The following study is designed to help you develop a better understanding of Christ's character through Scripture.[1] To help you think through each passage and consider what it means, we want you to paraphrase each passage in the space provided. The goal is not to "fill in the blanks," but to reflect on what these passages are saying. This will take some time. Be thorough with this exercise and think both about the meaning of each passage, and how to apply it in your daily experience.

■ Purpose

When Adam sinned, he brought both the burden and the penalty of sin upon all mankind. As a result, man is by nature rebellious against God, separated from Him and deserving of His righteous wrath.

> *Behold, the Lord's hand is not so short that it cannot save; neither is His ear so dull that it cannot hear.*
>
> *But your iniquities have made a separation between you and your God, and your sins have hidden His face from you, so that He does not hear.*
>
> Is. 59:1-2

• Paraphrase:

> *Or do you think lightly of the riches of His kindness and forbearance and patience, not knowing that the kindness of God leads you to repentance?*
>
> *But because of your stubbornness and unrepentant heart you are storing up wrath for yourself in the day of wrath and revelation of the righteous judgment of God . . . .*
>
> Rom. 2:4-5

• Paraphrase:

49

Having created man for fellowship with Him, God also created a plan whereby we can be united with Him. He sent His Son to die in our place, and through Christ's death, averted His wrath toward us. Therefore, we have fellowship with God.

> *For Christ also died for sins once for all, the just for the unjust, in order that He might bring us to God . . . .*
>
> 1 Pet. 3:18

• Paraphrase:

> *For the grace of God has appeared, bringing salvation to all men,*
> *instructing us to deny ungodliness and worldly desires and to live sensibly, righteously and godly in the present age,*
> *looking for the blessed hope and the appearing of the glory of our great God and Savior, Christ Jesus;*
> *who gave Himself for us, that He might redeem us from every lawless deed and purify for Himself a people for His own possession, zealous for good deeds.*
>
> Titus 2:11-14

• Paraphrase:

> *And there is salvation in no one else; for there is no other name under heaven that has been given among men, by which we must be saved.*
>
> Acts 4:12

• Paraphrase:

50

• From your paraphrases above, write a summary statement about the Lord's purpose:

■ **Unconditional love**
 Sacrificing His only Son's life on our behalf is overwhelming evidence of God's love for us.

> *By this the love of God was manifested in us, that God has sent His only begotten Son into the world so that we might live through Him.*
> *In this is love, not that we loved God, but that He loved us and sent His Son to be the propitiation for our sins.*
> 1 John 4:9-10

• Paraphrase:

> *For God so loved the world, that He gave His only begotten Son, that whoever believes in Him should not perish, but have eternal life.*
> *For God did not send the Son into the world to judge the world, but that the world should be saved through Him.*
> *He who believes in Him is not judged; he who does not believe has been judged already, because he has not believed in the name of the only begotten Son of God.*
> John 3:16-18

• Paraphrase:

> *. . . from Jesus Christ, the faithful witness, the first-born of the dead, and the ruler of the kings of the earth. To Him who loves us, and released us from our sins by His blood,*
>
> *and He has made us to be a kingdom, priests to His God and Father; to Him be the glory and the dominion forever and ever. Amen.*
>
> Rev. 1:5-6

• Paraphrase:

• From your paraphrases above, write a summary statement about God's unconditional love:

■ Complete forgiveness

Christ's death not only averted the wrath of God from those who believe in Him, but completely paid our debt of sin so that we are completely forgiven.

> *And when you were dead in your transgressions and the uncircumcision of your flesh, He made you alive together with Him, having forgiven us all our transgressions,*
>
> *having canceled out the certificate of debt consisting of decrees against us and which was hostile to us; and He has taken it out of the way, having nailed it to the cross.*
>
> Col. 2:13-14

• Paraphrase:

> *For while we were still helpless, at the right time Christ died for the ungodly.*
>
> *For one will hardly die for a righteous man; though perhaps for the good man someone would dare even to die.*

But God demonstrates His own love toward us, in that while we were yet sinners, Christ died for us.

Much more then, having now been justified by His blood, we shall be saved from the wrath of God through Him.

For if while we were enemies, we were reconciled to God through the death of His Son, much more, having been reconciled, we shall be saved by His life.

And not only this, but we also exult in God through our Lord Jesus Christ, through whom we have now received the reconciliation.

Rom. 5:6-11

• Paraphrase:

Because we are forgiven by God, we can forgive others.

... bearing with one another, and forgiving each other, whoever has a complaint against anyone; just as the Lord forgave you, so also should you.

Col. 3:13

• Paraphrase:

Now one of the Pharisees was requesting Him to dine with him. And He entered the Pharisee's house, and reclined at the table.

And behold, there was a woman in the city who was a sinner; and when she learned that He was reclining at the table in the Pharisee's house, she brought an alabaster vial of perfume, and standing behind Him at His feet, weeping, she began to wet His feet with her tears, and kept wiping them with the hair of her head, and kissing His feet, and anointing them with the perfume.

Now when the Pharisee who had invited Him saw this, he said to himself, "If this man were a prophet He would know who and what sort of person this woman is who is touching Him, that she is a sinner."

And Jesus answered and said to him, "Simon, I have something to say to you." And he replied, "Say it, Teacher."

"A certain moneylender had two debtors; one owed five hundred denarii, and the other fifty.

"When they were unable to repay, he graciously forgave them both. Which of them therefore will love him more?"

Simon answered and said, "I suppose the one whom he forgave more." And He said to him, "You have judged correctly."

And turning toward the woman, He said to Simon, "Do you see this woman? I entered your house; you gave Me no water for My feet, but she has wet My feet with her tears, and wiped them with her hair.

"You gave Me no kiss; but she, since the time I came in, has not ceased to kiss My feet.

"You did not anoint My head with oil, but she anointed My feet with perfume.

"For this reason I say to you, her sins, which are many, have been forgiven, for she loved much; but he who is forgiven little loves little."

And He said to her, "Your sins have been forgiven."

Luke 7:36-48

• Paraphrase:

• From your paraphrases above, write a summary statement about the Lord's complete forgiveness:

■ **Total Acceptance**

Christ's payment for our sins took away the barrier between Him and us so that we are now His beloved children and friends.

> *For you have not received a spirit of slavery leading to fear again, but you have received a spirit of adoption as sons by which we cry out, "Abba! Father!"*
> *The Spirit Himself bears witness with our spirit that we are children of God,*
> *and if children, heirs also, heirs of God and fellow heirs with Christ, if indeed we suffer with Him in order that we may also be glorified with Him.*
>
> Rom. 8:15-17

• Paraphrase:

> *. . . in order that He might redeem those who were under the Law, that we might receive the adoption as sons.*
> *And because you are sons, God has sent forth the Spirit of His Son into your hearts, crying, "Abba! Father!"*
> *Therefore you are no longer a slave, but a son; and if a son, then an heir through God.*
>
> Gal. 4:5-7

• Paraphrase:

Because we are totally accepted by God, we can unconditionally accept others.

Wherefore, accept one another, just as Christ also accepted us to the glory of God.

Rom. 15:7

• Paraphrase:

• Write a summary statement about God's total acceptance of us:

■ Authority and power

Christ has infinite authority and power. In His life and death on earth, He achieved our redemption. He defeated every temptation known to man (Heb. 2:14-15; 4:15), reconciled us to God (Matt. 26:28; Rom. 5:8) and triumphed over every evil power and authority (Col. 2:15). His resurrection proves that He has authority over death and that He is alive today (Luke 24:1-49; 1 Cor. 15:3-4). His ascension sealed His victory and ours (Mark 16:19; Luke 24:50-53; Acts 1:1-11). Scripture tells us that Jesus Christ is now seated at the right hand of God *in the heavenly places, far above all rule and authority and power and dominion, and every name that is named, not only in this age, but also in the one to come,* and that all things are in subjection to Him (Eph. 1:20-22).

Paraphrase the following passages about Christ's authority and power:

When He had disarmed the rulers and authorities, He made a public display of them, having triumphed over them through Him.

Col. 2:15

• Paraphrase:

And He is the image of the invisible God, the first-born of all creation.
For by Him all things were created, both in the heavens and on earth, visible and invisible, whether thrones or dominions or rulers or authorities—all things have been created by Him and for Him.

56

And He is before all things, and in Him all things hold together.

He is also the head of the body, the church; and He is the beginning, the first-born from the dead; so that He Himself might come to have first place in everything.

For it was the Father's good pleasure for all the fulness to dwell in Him,

and through Him to reconcile all things to Himself, having made peace through the blood of His cross; through Him, I say, whether things on earth or things in heaven.

Col. 1:15-20

• Paraphrase:

... in Him you have been made complete, and He is the head over all rule and authority ....

Col. 2:10

• Paraphrase:

Therefore also God highly exalted Him, and bestowed on Him the name which is above every name,

that at the name of Jesus every knee should bow, of those who are in heaven, and on earth, and under the earth,

and that every tongue should confess that Jesus Christ is Lord, to the glory of God the Father.

Phil. 2:9-11

• Paraphrase:

• Write a summary statement about the Lord's authority and power:

■ **Hope**

There is no hope of forgiveness and reconciliation to God apart from Christ.

> . . . remember that you were at that time separate from Christ, excluded from the commonwealth of Israel, and strangers to the covenants of promise, having no hope and without God in the world.
>
> Eph. 2:12

• Paraphrase:

His love, forgiveness and power give us hope for a new life.

> Blessed be the God and Father of our Lord Jesus Christ, who according to His great mercy has caused us to be born again to a living hope through the resurrection of Jesus Christ from the dead . . . .
>
> 1 Pet. 1:3

• Paraphrase:

> And we know that God causes all things to work together for good to those who love God, to those who are called according to His purpose.
>
> Rom. 8:28

• Paraphrase:

■ Write a summary statement about the hope of Christ:

■ **Faithfulness**

Christ is always faithful to do what He has promised.

> *No temptation has overtaken you but such as is common to man; and God is faithful, who will not allow you to be tempted beyond what you are able, but with the temptation will provide the way of escape also, that you may be able to endure it.*
>
> 1 Cor. 10:13

• Paraphrase:

> *Let us hold fast the confession of our hope without wavering, for He who promised is faithful . . . .*
>
> Heb. 10:23

• Paraphrase:

> *It is a trustworthy statement: For if we died with Him, we shall also live with Him;*
> *If we endure, we shall also reign with Him; if we deny Him, He also will deny us;*
> *If we are faithless, He remains faithful; for He cannot deny Himself.*
>
> 2 Tim. 2:11-13

• Paraphrase:

• Write a summary statement about the Lord's faithfulness:

■ **Wisdom**

The Lord has all knowledge and all wisdom. He knows what is best for us, and He will give us wisdom to know how we can honor Him in every situation.

But if any of you lacks wisdom, let him ask of God, who gives to all men generously and without reproach, and it will be given to him.

But let him ask in faith without any doubting, for the one who doubts is like the surf of the sea driven and tossed by the wind.

James 1:5-6

• Paraphrase:

For the word of the cross is to those who are perishing foolishness, but to us who are being saved it is the power of God.

For it is written, "I will destroy the wisdom of the wise, and the cleverness of the clever I will set aside."

Where is the wise man? Where is the scribe? Where is the debater of this age? Has not God made foolish the wisdom of the world?

For since in the wisdom of God the world through its wisdom did not come to know God, God was well-pleased through the foolishness of the message preached to save those who believe.

For indeed Jews ask for signs and Greeks search for wisdom;

but we preach Christ crucified, to Jews a stumbling block, and to Gentiles foolishness,

but to those who are the called, both Jews and Greeks, Christ the power of God and the wisdom of God.

Because the foolishness of God is wiser than men, and the weakness of God is stronger than men.

For consider your calling, brethren, that there were not many wise according to the flesh, not many mighty, not many noble;

but God has chosen the foolish things of the world to shame the wise, and God has chosen the weak things of the world to shame the things which are strong . . . .

1 Cor. 1:18-27

• Paraphrase:

> *"For My thoughts are not your thoughts, neither are your ways My ways,"* declares the Lord.
> *"For as the heavens are higher than the earth, so are My ways higher than your ways, and My thoughts than your thoughts."*
>
> Is. 55:8-9

• Paraphrase:

> *Therefore be careful how you walk, not as unwise men, but as wise,*
> *making the most of your time, because the days are evil.*
> *So then do not be foolish, but understand what the will of the Lord is.*
> *And do not get drunk with wine, for that is dissipation, but be filled with the Spirit,*
> *speaking to one another in psalms and hymns and spiritual songs, singing and making melody with your heart to the Lord;*
> *always giving thanks for all things in the name of our Lord Jesus Christ to God, even the Father;*
> *and be subject to one another in the fear of Christ.*
>
> Eph. 5:15-21

• Paraphrase:

• Write a summary statement about the Lord's wisdom:

■ Which passage in each section has been most meaningful to you? List the passage and describe why it is meaningful.

• Purpose

• Unconditional love

• Complete forgiveness

• Total acceptance

• Authority and power

• Hope

• Faithfulness

• Wisdom

Trusting in Christ

Augustine observed, "Thou hast made us for Thyself, O God, and the heart of man is restless until it finds its rest in Thee." God desires to have an intimate relationship with us, and He has given us a provision for continual access to Him through His Son, Jesus Christ (John 3:16-17; Heb. 2:17).

Are you trusting in your own abilities to earn acceptance with God, or are you trusting in the death of Christ to pay for your sins and the resurrection of Christ to give you new life? Take a moment to reflect on this question: On a scale of 0-100 percent, how sure are you that you would spend eternity with God if you died today? An answer of less than 100 percent may indicate that you are trusting, at least in part, in yourself. You may be thinking, *Isn't it arrogant to say that I am 100 percent sure?* Indeed, it would be arrogance if you were trusting in yourself—your abilities, your actions and good deeds—to earn your salvation. However, if you are no longer trusting in your own efforts, but in the all-sufficient payment of Christ, then 100 percent certainty is a response of humility and thankfulness, not arrogance.

Reflect on a second question: If you were to die today and stand before God, and He were to ask you, "Why should I let you into heaven?" what would you tell Him? Would you mention your abilities, church attendance, kindness to others, Christian service, abstinence from a particular sin or some other good deed? Paul wrote to Titus:

> *But when the kindness of God our Savior and His love*
> *for mankind appeared,*
> *He saved us, not on the basis of deeds which we have*
> *done in righteousness, but according to His mercy . . . .*
> Titus 3:4-5

And to the Ephesians he wrote:

> *For by grace you have been saved through faith; and*
> *that not of yourselves, it is the gift of God;*
> *not as a result of works, that no one should boast.*
> Eph. 2:8-9

We must give up our own efforts to achieve righteousness and instead believe that Christ's death and resurrection alone are sufficient to pay for our sin and separation from God.

In Acts 16:31, Luke wrote, *. . . Believe in the Lord Jesus, and you shall be saved . . . .* Jesus said: *I am the way, and the truth, and the life; no one comes to the Father, but through Me* (John 14:6).

We receive Jesus by invitation. Scripture says:

> *But as many received Him, to them He gave the right to become children of God, even to those who believe in His name.*
>
> John 1:12

Take some time to reflect on the two questions we examined above. Reflect on God's love, which He has expressed to you by sending His only Son to die in your place. Read Luke 22:39-46. Consider the selfless sacrifice of Jesus to carry out this divine plan. Realize that if you were the only person to walk this earth, Jesus would have done this for you.

If you are not 100 percent sure that you would spend eternity with God if you died today, and if you are willing to trust in Christ and accept His payment for your sins, you may use this prayer to express your faith:

> *Lord Jesus, I need You. I want You to be my Savior and my Lord. I accept Your death on the cross as payment for my sins, and now entrust my life to Your care. Thank You for forgiving me and for giving me a new life. Thank You for the new life that is now mine through You. Please help me grow in my understanding of Your love and power so that my life will bring glory and honor to You. Amen.*

_____(date) _____ (signature)

If you have placed your trust in Jesus Christ prior to reading this, consider reaffirming your faith and commitment to serve Him. You may do so by using this prayer:

> *Lord Jesus, I need You and thank You that I am Yours. I confess that I have sinned against You, and ask You to "create in me a clean heart, and renew a steadfast spirit*

within me" (Ps 51:10). I renew my commitment to serve
You. Thank You for loving me and for forgiving me. Please
give me Your strength and wisdom to continue growing in
You so that my life can bring glory and honor to You. Amen.

_____(date) _____ (signature)

It is important to understand that trusting in Christ does not guarantee an instantaneous deliverance from eating-disordered behavior or from any other problem in life. However, it does mean that you are forgiven for your rebellion against God; that you are restored to a relationship with Him that will last throughout eternity; and that you will receive His unconditional love and acceptance, as well as His strength and wisdom, as you continue to grow in recovery.

As a result of our trust in Christ, we can depend on the many facts and promises in God's Word. Facts are truths that are already true of us; promises are statements that we know will be fulfilled because of the trustworthiness of God. Here is a very short list of both:

Facts from God's Word
You are completely forgiven by God (Rom. 3:19-25; Col. 2:13-14).
You are righteous and pleasing to God (2 Cor. 5:21).
You are totally accepted by God (Col. 1:19-22).
You are deeply loved by God (1 John 4:9-10).
You are absolutely complete in Christ (2 Cor. 5:17; Col. 2:10).
The Holy Spirit dwells in you (Rom. 8:9-11).
You are God's child (Rom. 8:15-16).
You are a fellow heir with Christ (Rom. 8:17).
God works all things for good for those who love Him (Rom. 8:28).

Promises from God's Word
Christ will never leave us (Matt. 28:20; Heb. 13:5).
He will abundantly provide for our needs (Phil. 4:19).
We will be in heaven with Him (John 14:1-3).
We will reign with Him (2 Tim. 2:12).
He will strengthen us (Is. 40:29).
He will give us His peace (John 14:27).
He will accomplish His purposes (1 Thess. 5:24).
He will enable us to give generously (2 Cor. 9:6-11).
We will be persecuted (John 15:18-21).

For Additional Reflection and Application

We have entitled this step, "My Saving Decision." It is interesting to think about what *save* means. Two words are used in the New Testament Greek (the language in which the New Testament was originally written) for "healing," which is what we are seeking in our quest for freedom from eating disorders. Therapy is derived from the first word, *therapauo*, and means, "to facilitate the healing process." This is the word which was used to describe acts of miraculous healing performed by the Holy Spirit through people like the Apostles. They "facilitated" the healing process by their availability, by interacting with the person to be healed, by prayer, by the laying on of hands, etc. But when Jesus Himself healed, the word used was *sozo*, meaning "to directly act to rescue, save and deliver." What a wonderful way to combine *save* and *heal* into one concept—which is what is involved in step 3. We make a responsible choice to trust the God we have been discovering since our decision to believe that He could restore us in step 2; He responds by saving and healing us.

Several years ago, a young woman who had bulimia nervosa shared the following Scripture with regard to what she was coming to understand about her eating disorder, her recovery and the saving, healing grace of Jehovah Rapha, "The Lord who heals":

> *. . . The hungry soul He has filled with what is good.*
> *. . . He brought them out of darkness and the shadow of death, and broke their bands apart.*
> *. . . He has shattered gates of bronze, and cut bars of iron asunder.*
> *Their souls abhorred all kinds of food; and they drew near to the gates of death.*
> *Then they cried out to the Lord in their trouble . . .*
> *He sent His word and healed them, and delivered them from their destructions.*
>
> Ps. 107:9b, 14, 16, 18-20

Making the responsible choice to trust God moment–by–moment, day–by–day, begins our new life of healing, growth and renewal. When troubles arise, our response needs to be the same as here at step 3: *to turn our lives over to God through Jesus Christ.* When circumstances threaten to overwhelm us and our eating disorders beckon us to return: *turn our lives over to God through Jesus Christ.* When we need to make an important personal decision: *turn our lives over to God through Jesus Christ.* When we are tempted to worry about others or ourselves, when anxiety and fear threaten to overtake us, when we rise with the morning's light and retire into the quiet of night—again, our decision must be the same: *to turn our lives over to God through Jesus Christ.*

> *Humble yourselves, therefore, under God's mighty*
> *hand, that he may lift you up in due time.*
> *Cast all your anxiety on him because he cares for you.*
> 1 Pet. 5:6-7, NIV

Steps 1 through 3 serve as preparation for the work we must do in recovery. To move beyond this point will require continued courage. As Joshua prepared to assume the former leadership of Moses and bring the nation of Israel into the Promised Land, he undoubtedly felt anxious at the enormity of the task before him. God first reminded him, *I will never leave you nor forsake you* (Josh. 1:5), a promise Jesus later repeated when He said, *And surely I am with you always, to the very end of the age* (Matt. 28:20, both NIV). God then told Joshua three times, *Be strong and courageous* (Josh. 1:6-7, 9). In step 4, we will learn exactly what *courageous* means, and how indeed to be "strong and courageous." In preparation, it may be useful to consider the words of an old hymn:

> *Fear not, I am with thee, O be not dismayed,*
> *For I am thy God and will still give thee aid;*
> *I'll strengthen thee, help thee, and cause thee to stand,*
> *Upheld by My righteous, omnipotent hand.*

> *When through the deep waters I call thee to go,*
> *The rivers of sorrow shall not overflow;*
> *For I will be with thee, thy troubles to bless,*
> *And sanctify to thee thy deepest distress.*

> *When through fiery trials thy pathway shall lie,*
> *My grace, all-sufficient, shall be thy supply;*
> *The flame shall not hurt thee; I only design*
> *Thy dross to consume, and thy gold to refine.*

The soul that on Jesus hath leaned for repose,
I will not, I will not desert to his foes;
That soul, though all hell should endeavor to shake,
I'll never, no never, no never forsake.[2]

Step Four
My Face-to-Face Encounter

We make a searching, courageous moral inventory of ourselves.

Let us examine and probe our ways,
and let us return to the Lord.

Lam. 3:40

Socrates once said, "The unexamined life is not worth living." Many people understand *self-examination* to mean either "self-absorption" or "self-condemnation." Step 4, however, refers to taking an *inventory*. A shopkeeper takes an inventory of his store so that he will know what he has in stock, what is damaged or outdated and needs replacing, what needs to be ordered and what new items need to be put in stock. An inventory of one's self is simply a thorough in-house survey. It is a complete assessment and evaluation of one's good and bad traits, strengths and weaknesses, assets and liabilities.

Far from being a means of self-condemnation or self-abasement, a "searching and courageous moral inventory" is a tool which can provide help for developing healthy self-esteem, as well as a plan for growth and maturation. It exposes hazards which may provoke relapse to eating-disordered behavior. It highlights the individual strengths and gifts we possess in our uniqueness as persons whom God has created—all of which will support our recovery.

A moral inventory also exposes our weaknesses. Looking at the negative aspects of our personalities and behavior is difficult for those of us with perfectionistic tendencies, the reason why courage is so necessary.

Courage has nothing to do with *fearlessness*. It was an attitude of fearlessness that governed the insanity of our eating-disordered behavior! Unfortunately, many Christians have the mistaken notion that fear is ungodly and morally wrong. Certainly, secular society frowns upon fear; consequently, most of us have grown up being afraid of fear. In fact, it is precisely this truth that Scripture references in a passage which frequently is misquoted:

69

For God did not give us a spirit of timidity (fear of fear)
but a spirit of power, of love and of self-discipline.

2 Tim. 1:7, NIV

Fear is an important and healthy emotion; it prompts us to look both ways before crossing the street. In like manner, fear gives us the incentive to face our defects of character and begin the process of changing them, so that they do not provide the golden pathway for relapse.

It takes courage to face those aspects of our personalities and behavior that need to be improved or eliminated. Sometimes it is equally difficult to accept our strengths and virtues. Because of our low self-esteem, we tend to reject what is good and see only what we dislike about ourselves. This is a form of perfectionism, and we can do without it, thank you very much!

Trying to hide our flaws, both from others and ourselves, may seem like a good solution, but ultimately, anything we keep in secret gains increased power over us because of the secrecy. This is due to a number of factors, one being that when we hide something about ourselves from others, we usually invest a great amount of energy in maintaining appearances. As time passes, keeping the secret hidden demands increasing amounts of our anxious preoccupation and consumes more of our attention and resources. Our "investment" in self-protection gives the secret more power over us. In addition to the above, secrecy prevents us from facing the consequences of our behavior squarely and leads to an inner sense of despair. Thus the cycle of addictive behavior continues, both as an act of irresponsibility and an act of self-medicated relief. Proverbs 28:13 tells us,

He who conceals his transgressions will not prosper,
but he who confesses and forsakes them will find
compassion.

Denial is an inability or unwillingness to recognize problems, or perceive reality, in and around one's self. It is an inner defense mechanism many of us use to block concepts that produce painful emotions. In psychological terms, denial is referenced as a "psychotic ego defense" (*psychotic* is another way of saying *insane;* an *ego defense* refers to a way of thinking or behaving which protects the individual from feeling or experiencing an unwelcome emotion, or acknowledging a fact about him- or herself or others). We deny that we have a particular flaw or have committed a certain sin (or have an eating disorder) in an attempt to (1) protect ourselves from facing real and/or perceived implications and consequences of the problem and to (2) prevent others from knowing about it. Denial is truly "psychotic," because it is founded on one or more delusional beliefs, unconnected with reality, which we seek to convince others and ourselves is true.

In step 2, we decided to seek God for restoration of our sanity through Jesus Christ. To replace denial with courageous honesty often may be painful, but it returns management of our lives to us because it robs our character defects of the power that secrecy gives them. The emptiness which we tried to fill with compulsive food behaviors now can be filled with God's truth. This opens the door for freedom, for Jesus said, *You will know the truth, and the truth will set you free* (John 8:32).

When we discover patterns of sin within us, what do we do? We confess them, seek God's forgiveness and ask Him to give us a heart of repentance.

■ Paraphrase the following passage:

> *If we claim to be without sin, we deceive ourselves, and the truth is not in us.*
> *If we confess our sins, He is faithful and just and will forgive us our sins and purify us from all unrighteousness.*
>
> 1 John 1:8-9, NIV

• Paraphrase:

• What does it mean to "confess our sins"?

> *For we do not have a high priest who is unable to sympathize with our weaknesses, but we have one who has been tempted in every way, just as we are—yet was without sin.*
> *Let us then approach the throne of grace with confidence, so that we may receive mercy and find grace to help us in our time of need.*
>
> Heb. 4:15-16, NIV

71

■ According to these two passages, what is God's response to our honesty when we openly disclose to Him and to ourselves our negative inventory?

• How is this different from the responses others have given you in the past?

• How does this differ from the way you typically respond when others disclose negative aspects about themselves to you?

Character Gamesmanship

The complex maneuvering in which we often engage to control our lives and others' can be called *gamesmanship*. Those of us with eating disorders are crafty gamesters all too often; unfortunately, these are games in which everyone loses, and the only way to win is not to play. What is the best way to block a punch in boxing? Take up tennis instead! In other words, the only way to keep from being a loser is to avoid the game altogether.

Here are some typical games and their corresponding solutions:

Game	Solution
Dishonesty	Honesty
Resentment	Forgiveness
Self-Pity (Dejection)	Gratitude
Impatience and Impulsiveness	Patience
False Pride/False Humility	Humility
Destructive Anger	Constructive Anger
Fear	Trust
Criticism	Love

Notice that each of these "games" has an alternative which turns our attention from self-absorption outward to others. Perhaps you already are beginning to see the Holy Spirit beginning this change in you— congratulations! Let's examine some of these "games" more closely.

Dishonesty: How to Be a Successful Coward

Whoa there! Does that seem a bit too blunt? Get used to it! Only relentless honesty and courage will help here. A *coward* is not someone with a lot of fear, but someone who will not face what he or she fears most. We fear our defects of character (and even the idea that we have them at all!), but we can ask God for courage to show us what we need to change. So let's try that again.

Dishonesty: How to Be a Successful Coward

Dishonesty basically is the sin of avoiding truth, and represents *character cowardice*. Those of us whose lives have been characterized by eating disorders struggle with dishonesty, especially as it relates to exposing any truth about which we might be uncomfortable or fearful. Many times, a tendency toward dishonesty arises out of a poor self-esteem which insists that our true selves are thoroughly unacceptable. This perpetuates our need to hide from the scrutiny of others, including God and ourselves.

Dishonesty may be characterized by any of the following:

- Hiding/Secretiveness
- Masking
- Excuse-Making
- Half-Truths
- "Little White Lies"

- Phoniness
- "Forgetting" Promises
- Con-Jobs
- Manipulation
- Minimizing

■ Do you try to make sure no one knows the "real you"? If so, explain how:

• Does the thought of having others know about your eating disorder (even "significant others") make you feel "paranoid"? If so, explain why you have this fear:

■ Do you look for others to blame, or seek to excuse yourself, rather than face up to a mistake, error or transgression you have committed? If so, explain:

• Describe any incidents in which you've tried to "protect yourself" by telling only partial truths:

• How have you tried to minimize your dishonesty by convincing yourself and/or others that you only have told a "little white lie"?

■ Do you try to impress others with the idea that you are someone or something other than who or what you really are, because you believe that your life would otherwise be considered unimportant or have little meaning? If so, give an example and explain why you feel this way:

■ Do you have a tendency to avoid necessary tasks or promises by pleading "forgetfulness"? If so, give an example of this behavior and explain why you think you've acted this way:

Honesty

When we were bound to our compulsion, our egos—already frail—couldn't stand up to the truth about ourselves. We were too afraid of what we might see if we looked honestly at our behavior. But now that we're making improvements in our lives, we can afford to give ourselves an honest evaluation. We begin by taking this inventory.

Being truthful is easier now because there's less to hide. We no longer are compelled to hoard food, shoplift, sneak around to purge, hide laxatives or wear bulky clothing to hide our body size and weight.

If we have chosen involvement in a support group or treatment, we are discovering that many others have faced, or are facing, some of the same problems we have experienced. This helps us to be genuine and know that we no longer have to swallow our anger and fear, and try to convince others that we never have problems, that all is well. We can be honest with others and ourselves.

Finally, we are beginning to realize that we can always be honest with God. He made us. He knows our every thought, our every word, our every action. And He loves us anyway. His love for us is unconditional. What a relief to have One with whom we can be *totally* honest!

■ Name some areas in your life in which you now feel free to be honest:

■ What factors and people encourage you to be more honest about your life?

■ Has recovery been a source of help to you in becoming more honest? If so, explain:

■ In what aspects of your life have you had the most difficulty in being honest, and why?

■ How does being honest affect your self-esteem?

■ Paraphrase Ps. 139:1-6:

■ Does realizing that the Lord already knows everything about you—both good and bad—help you to be more honest? Why or why not?

Resentment: How to Be a Successful Abuser

Resentment is a refusal to let go of anger at some past harm. Often, it results in a punitive attitude toward the person who offended us—and sometimes, toward others as well. Resentment generally makes abusers out of us. Through resentment, we often find ourselves becoming like the very ones we despise. In addition, it may cause us to resist the basic and important requirements for healthy lifestyles and relationships as a result of passive-aggressive resistance to authority. Any of the following may be indicative of an underlying attitude of resentment:

- "I forgot." *(I really didn't want to . . .")*
- Gossip, slander, defamation
- "Justifiable" grudge-bearing
- Self-righteous indignation
- Plotting or seeking revenge/retaliation
- Chronic lateness
- Long-term nursing of anger
- Avoidance/silent treatment
- Blame
- Sarcasm

■ Do you tend to carry grudges? Are you unforgiving?

■ How have you expressed resentment toward others?
- Have you ever hidden your anger toward others through "humorous barbs," or sarcasm? If so, explain:

- Have you ever talked about the wrongs or misfortunes of others because you were secretly pleased about their problems? Explain:

- Have you ever looked for subtle ways to "get even" with someone? Explain:

• Explain any incident in which you've given the "silent treatment" to someone with whom you've been angry, punishing that person by refusing to talk with him or her:

• Describe any other ways in which you've expressed resentment toward another person:

■ Do you ever feel contempt toward authority figures—even those whom you do not know?

■ Read Matt. 18:21-35. What does this passage teach about withholding forgiveness from others?

Forgiveness

Forgiveness means giving up our perceived right to punish the one who has offended us. One author has written that three elements are essential to the process of forgiving: an injury, a debt resulting from the injury and a cancellation of the debt.[1] However, rather than recognize an injury and count the cost we've incurred as a result of it, many of us tend to minimize (or even negate) its value and excuse the offender: *She couldn't help it*, we may tell ourselves, or, *He didn't really mean to hurt me*. Responses like these may sound noble, but they obstruct honesty and consequently block our ability to extend complete forgiveness.

Discounting the magnitude of both our sin and Christ's payment for it on the cross also contributes to our inability to forgive others (Luke 7:36-50). In addition, many of us are convinced that we have to earn forgiveness from God. We may therefore punish those who offend us in an attempt to ensure that they "pay for" their sins against us.

Again, forgiveness is an informed decision to bear the pain of another's offense without demanding that he or she be punished for it. This does not mean that we are to overlook or accept unacceptable behavior. The process of forgiving may include talking with the person who has hurt us about his or her behavior and/or allowing that person to experience any negative consequences produced by his or her behavior. This enables the offender to understand at least some of the effects of the wrongdoing. Such an experience may not prompt change in the offender's behavior nor serve as the basis of change in our relationship with him or her. However, regardless of another person's response, we still are responsible for forgiving anyone who offends us.

Why should we forgive?

- *God commands us to forgive others through Jesus Christ.* "And whenever you stand praying, forgive, if you have anything against anyone . . . " (Mark 11:25).
- *We have been forgiven by God through Jesus Christ.* "And be kind to one another, tender-hearted, forgiving each other, just as God in Christ also has forgiven you" (Eph. 4:32).
- *An unforgiving spirit hurts us.* Not forgiving often leads to suppressed hurt and anger. Repressing negative emotions affects our every relationship and leads to bitterness, depression and alienation. This deadly combination can turn the eating-disordered person back to compulsive food behavior.

■ From step 3, describe the forgiveness you have in Christ. Explain what it is, how it was given and how this affects you.

• Define *forgiveness*:

• How has God extended forgiveness to you through Christ?

• How does this affect you?

■ What persons have offended you or harmed you? What did they do to you?

Persons   **Offenses**

■ What would it mean to release each person from the penalty he or she owes you?

Persons   **Results of Forgiveness**

■ Have you forgiven any of them already? If so, explain how:

Persons   **Forgiveness**

■ What have been the results of extending forgiveness...
  • For you?

  • For the offender(s)?

■ How can you tell that you've forgiven someone?

■ What are some of the emotional, relational, spiritual and mental consequences of unforgivingness...

  • For you?

  • For the offender(s)?

■ Paraphrase Col. 3:13:

Self-Pity: How to Be a Life-Long Victim

Self-pity often arises out of a significant truth—we have been deeply hurt in life and our wounds ache due to lack of attention and care. There is nothing wrong with acknowledging the fact that we have been hurt; nor is it wrong to allow ourselves to experience the pain associated with that hurt.

However, when we prolong that experience, we sometimes fall into a "pity trap." In so doing, we may perceive ourselves as victims to the extent that we deny to others and ourselves our capacity for wrong doing. We may become immobilized so that our lives become characterized by passivity and blame. Self-pity prompts us to control, trap and manipulate others in an attempt to have them do for us what we need to do for ourselves: to face the truth, accept it, deal with it and get on with a productive life. Common characteristics associated with self-pity include:

- Projection: "I feel bad . . . it's your (his/her) fault."
- Denial: "I never did anything wrong." "I never get anything right."
- Avoiding responsibility by reciting a litany of past hurts.
- Avoiding responsibility by pleading physical distress.
- Reading the "whine list."
- "You're the only friend I have/who understands me."
- Controlling others by making them feel important.

■ How have you avoided responsibility for your negative feelings or circumstances?

- Do you ever refuse to acknowledge that you may have done something wrong? If so, why?

• Have you ever sought the pity of others for your inability to achieve? Explain:

• Have you relied on physical complaints or illnesses in order to escape responsibility? If so, explain:

• Have you ever avoided taking responsibility for yourself due to past abuse or some other misfortune you've suffered? If so, how has this doubled the burden you've carried?

• Have you used profuse praise or thankfulness, emphasizing how indispensable another person is to you, in order to motivate that person to take care of you and/or protect you? If so, explain:

Gratitude

As our mental, emotional, physical and spiritual well-being is gradually restored, we become more thankful, realizing that the changes we and other people are beginning to see within us are the gift of God through Christ.

Our gratitude motivates us to share this news with other people. Also, because we are starting to feel better about ourselves, and are less preoccupied with our well-being, we begin wanting to exercise responsibility and share our resources with other people: our time, energies, talents, and sometimes, even our finances.

Some of us may be surprised to discover that giving of ourselves brings us great satisfaction. . . . *freely you received, freely give* (Matt. 10:8).

■ Complete the following statement: *Contentment comes...*

■ List the people, situations and things for which you are thankful:

■ How are you sharing...
  • Your resources?

  • Your possessions?

  • Yourself?

■ How is gratitude an anecdote to the behavior that accompanies prolonged self-pity?

Impatience and Impulsiveness

I want what I want—now! All addictions have the characteristic of impatience; we have no tolerance for delayed gratification. We felt anxious and trembled as we impatiently waited for the three pizzas to be ready and given to us; we became angry as the person on the other side of the drive-through window laboriously counted our change. This attitude carried over into our relationships. We barked out orders, and by our actions and attitudes, demanded that those around us "shape up" and "get in line" *NOW!* We were impatient at work, always hurrying to meet deadlines, hoping to prove ourselves and move to the top. Annoyance as a result of impatience led to still more anxiety and gave the eating disorder even more work to do. Impatience carried over into other aspects of our lives. Many of us spent money we didn't have, stole food that wasn't ours and lied to those we love—all because we had no patience.

■ In what ways are you impatient or impulsive?

■ What is your understanding of your need for immediacy?

■ What people and circumstances seem to provoke feelings of impatience within you?

People   **Circumstances**

■ Using the list made in the above response, what do you usually say and do at these times?

People/Circumstances   **Response**

■ Name some consequences of impatience and impulsiveness in . . .
  • Your schoolwork/vocation:

  • Your relationships:

  • Your eating behavior:

■ How have the above affected your self-esteem?

■ Paraphrase Eph.4:1-3:

Patience

Recovery provides an opportunity for us to learn patience. Gone is the immediate escape and gratification once provided by our eating disorder. Gone for many of us is the sense of security we experienced when others were acting as our rescuers and caretakers. The result is that we are gradually recognizing our limitations and are beginning to slow down a little. In so doing, we are exercising patience.

In recovery, we demonstrate patience each time we outlast an urge to resort to our eating-disordered behaviors. We exercise patience when we begin to control our spending and other habits. We develop patience as we look for God's will and wait for His direction. Patience allows us to receive more enjoyment from others. And to give more enjoyment to them.

Patience is a form of self-control; self-control is a demonstration of the Holy Spirit's work within us (Gal. 5:22-23).

■ How might God's grace, love, forgiveness and acceptance help you overcome impatience?

■ How are you applying (or how can you apply) these characteristics of God to others and to yourself in the circumstances you listed in your Impatience Inventory?

■ Name some possible results in your life and relationships as you learn to be patient through experiencing God's love, forgiveness and acceptance:

■ From Phil. 4:5-7, how can the Lord help you to be more peaceful and patient?

False Pride/False Humility

Among the many ailments ascribed to our eating disorder, false pride and false humility are among the most detrimental. These are black-or-white perspectives in which one oscillates between being the "Great I Am" and the "Poor Me."

False pride obstructs recovery because it is based on the notion that we don't need the help of God or other people, thank you; we are self-sufficient. Those who manifest this trait do so by an unwillingness to seek help; by an unwillingness to be wrong and apologize; by an unwillingness to admit powerlessness over any habit, including an eating disorder.

False humility is self-devaluation. It blocks recovery because it is founded on negative conclusions from past experiences, rather than on an accurate appraisal of our self-worth in God's eyes. False humility is often characterized by self-condemnation, passivity, fear, a sense of hopelessness and defeat.

The apostle Paul wrote the Romans: *I say to every man among you not to think more highly of himself than he ought to think; but to think so as to have sound judgment, as God has allotted to each a measure of faith* (Rom. 12:3).

■ On what occasions have you thought of yourself as the "Great I Am"?

• Why do you think you've sometimes felt this way about yourself?

• How has false pride hurt you and your relationships?

• In what situations have you experienced fear, a sense of hopelessness or defeat?

• Why do you think you've felt this way?

■ In what kinds of situations do you tend to act passively, and why?

• How have these feelings and actions affected you and your relationships?

■ Paraphrase Rom. 12:3.

Humility

Our humility began with the acknowledgment that we are powerless over our eating disorder. It continues to take a place within our lives as we daily submit ourselves to God for continued restoration.

Having received His beneficial help during these initial stages of recovery, we have realized the need we have for support from other people. When we are feeling out of sorts or tempted to indulge in eating-disordered thinking or behavior, we call on others or attend a support meeting. The fellowship we find there helps to meet the needs we once tried to fill with our food compulsion.

By listening to other people who share our predicament, we realize that everyone has strengths and weaknesses—including us. And we realize that it's okay to be human, to be genuine with other people and with God.

■ Paraphrase Phil. 2:3-4:

■ Define *humility* in your own words:

■ Are you practicing humility? If so, how?

■ Does the idea of being humble frighten and/or disgust you? If so, how and why?

■ How can humility be a sign of objectivity and strength:

■ How can (or how does) practicing humility affect . . .
  • Your life:

  • Your relationship with God:

  • Your relationships with other people:

91

Destructive Anger

Anger is a God-given emotional response that we all experience on occasion. Surrendered to God and used wisely, with control, it can have a positive result. Unaided and unimpeded, however, anger can have tragic consequences.

Anger can be a response to unmet expectations, irritation or frustration when things don't go our way or a demonstration of hostility when someone has a different opinion. Anger also can be a defensive response to a hurtful attack or to a real or perceived threat to one's self-esteem or well-being.

As with all other emotions, it is okay to *feel* angry. What we do with it is something else. Many of us use our anger destructively rather than constructively.

Destructive anger can be expressed outwardly or inwardly; either way, it can result in depression, suspicion and a low sense of self-worth. Examples of destructive anger are verbal abuse (screaming, criticism, fault-finding), physical abuse, teasing, sarcasm and murder. Silence, neglect and withdrawal also can be destructive expressions of anger.

The apostle Paul wrote: *Be angry, and yet do not sin; do not let the sun go down on your anger, and do not give the devil an opportunity* (Eph. 4:26-27).

Destructive anger can have catastrophic effects on our recovery. Expressed outwardly, it can alienate us from others and drive a wedge between God and us. Without these sources of help, we are likely to return to our addiction to fill the void of emptiness in our lives. Anger turned inward is also dangerous. As people with eating disorders, we have a low tolerance for the burdening effects of repressed anger. If anger is not dealt with constructively, we may return to compulsive behavior for relief from these negative emotions.

■ From the above, how do you usually express anger, and why?

■ Are these usually inward or outward expressions?

■ Do particular people or situations seem to trigger your anger? If so, describe:

■ Cite three examples of how destructive anger has affected you and your relationships:

• SITUATION:

• Response:

• Result:

• SITUATION:

• Response:

• Result:

• SITUATION:

• Response:

• Result:

Constructive Anger

In recovery, we begin to discover ways we can channel anger into positive action. Because we are releasing our grip on denial, we can more often admit feelings of anger, first to ourselves and then to God.

The biblical King David offers a good illustration of handling unwelcome emotions like anger positively. Before his induction as king of Israel, David was continually assaulted by his outraged, half-crazed father-in-law, Saul, who was then ruler over Israel, and who wanted to kill David. Under constant attack, David had every reason to be defensive and angry. Yet David was able both to honor Saul and to gain victory over his potentially destructive emotions because he had learned to express those emotions to God (see 1 Sam. 26:1-25, Ps. 42 and 58).

David used his anger constructively; it drove him to his knees. Once we can admit that we are angry, we can ask God for His direction in our response. We can call our sponsor or a friend who can add objectivity to our situation. Then, if necessary, we can confront the offender with an attitude of love.

Constructive anger can give us the momentum we need to detach from a manipulative person or a harmful situation. It can give us the incentive to confront someone in love; it can motivate us to stop abusing our bodies with eating-disordered behavior.

As we progress in recovery, we gradually learn that anger is a gift from God, intended to compel us to provide loving correction and to confront the evils which threaten His purposes. We can only begin to do this as He intends by seeking His direction before we make our response.

■ What are some examples of using anger constructively?

■ Have you been able to use your anger constructively? If so, describe three situations with the results of having done this in each.
  • SITUATION:

  • Response:

• Result:

• SITUATION:

• Response:

• Result:

• SITUATION:

• Response:

• Result:

■ Paraphrase Eph. 4:26-27:

■ How can you use anger for godly purposes in your life?

Fear

Fear is a God-given emotional response to the awareness of danger. In proper perspective and in certain situations, it has an appropriate place in all of our lives. Fear can prompt us to make decisions necessary for survival. We exercise fear wisely when we warn children to avoid playing with matches, to stay away from strangers and to look both ways when crossing the street. A constructive response to fear includes taking precautions against disease, theft and natural disasters.

When we were involved in compulsive food behavior, however, fear usually played a dictatorial role in our lives, and our response to it was more often destructive than constructive.

Fear blocked our ability to love; we limited our social involvement. Fear motivated us to avoid risks of failure and rejection, and relegated us to a need to be in control; we abused our bodies and others; we scheduled our lives around our food behavior, some of us hiding food, some of us dreading possible arrest for shoplifting—all in an attempt to gain control and security.

Even in recovery, we still may consumed by fear. We may be unable to sleep at night for fear of possible failure in our work or school performance. Afraid of failing, we may avoid anything new that involves risk, including parties or other social situations which involve food. A fear of rejection may cause us to avoid meeting people and going to support-group meetings.

Feeling afraid is okay. But it need not consume us. Recovery gives us an opportunity to learn how to examine fear objectively and utilize it constructively; to recognize it as a signal to correct something that's wrong within us or around us. It's helpful to talk with a trusted friend about our fears to see if they're reasonable. It's also wise to take them to God. He doesn't want us to be imprisoned by fear: *For God has not given us a spirit of timidity, but of power and love and discipline* (2 Tim. 1:7). *His perfect love casts out fear* (1 John 4:18).

■ Read Rom. 8:15. How are slavery and adoption contrasted?

■ What does each produce?
• Slavery:

- Adoption:

■ Whom or what do you fear most, and why?

■ How does fear control...
  - Your attitudes?

  - Your actions?

  - Your relationships?

  - Your sense of freedom?

Trust

As we are released from the tyranny of our compulsive food behavior, we develop the courage to acknowledge our fears and move forward with our lives in spite of them. As we do, we exercise trust and discover truth.

Many of our fears are actually rooted in lies. For example, many of us were convinced that we would meet with catastrophe without our addictive food behavior. Now we are learning that while we are challenged by the many facets of recovery, its benefits far outweigh the short-term gratification we once received from compulsively abusing food. That's the truth. We had to exercise some faith to find it.

Faith was also required when we placed our trust in Jesus Christ. Now we are discovering that He can do a better job of directing our lives than we ever could have done. By developing trust in Him, we begin to learn that we can afford to take the risks of getting to know some people and trying some new things. Fellowship is helpful to our recovery. So is knowing that if we're rejected, He still accepts us, and if we fail, He still loves us.

We learn that because no human is consistent enough to merit our complete trust, we can accept people and trust God. Scripture tells us that trusting in God is the way to experience peace: *The steadfast of mind Thou wilt keep in perfect peace, because he trusts in Thee* (Is. 26:3).

■ Read Ps. 27:1-3, 13-14. Describe David's trust in the Lord:

■ Contrast the effects of fear and trust in a person's life:

Fear   **Trust**

98

■ How do we develop trust?

■ How has Christ shown Himself to be trustworthy?

■ What have you trusted Him to be or do for you?

Criticism

Here, we are not thinking of the constructive advice we offer when asked, but that negative judgment of others and ourselves that is rooted in pride, in our need to be perfect or to be perceived as such.

Usually, criticism takes the form of verbal abuse, but sometimes, it can be more subtle, masked in sarcasm or silence.

There are many reasons why we are critical. One is that we often see others as reflections of ourselves. Criticism thus becomes a form of control which motivates others to conform to our standards.

We put other people down to elevate ourselves. This usually is the result of a low sense of self-worth and the false belief: *Those who fail are unworthy of love and deserve to be punished.*

Sometimes we are critical because we truly believe others need our guidance. We perceive that our correction will be beneficial to them. Later, we are surprised to realize that these people avoid us because our habit of "correcting" has been more destructive than constructive to them.

Scripture admonishes us to . . . *encourage one another, and build up one another* . . . (1 Thess. 5:11), and tells us that we are to . . . *love one another, for love is from God . . . if God so loved us, we also ought to love one another* (1 John 4:7,11).

As two writers have said: "People need love, especially when they don't deserve it,"[2] and, "He who seeks a friend without a fault remains without one."[3]

We would do well to remember to pray for others as often as we are tempted to criticize them.

■ Why do you criticize other people? What results do you expect?

■ In what ways do you communicate criticism?

■ How does a critical attitude affect your relationships, including your relationship with God?

• How does it affect you?

Love

When we consider love, we may think of the warm exuberance, queasiness, restlessness and sense of anticipation we feel toward another person when "falling in love." Fortunately, these emotional feelings, experienced at the onset of attraction, do not comprise the full context of love because feelings like these tend to ebb and flow.

God ordained love to be a lasting attitude comprised of action, and He who goes before us in all things has given us the example we are to follow in this area. John 3:16 says: "God *so loved* the world that He *gave* His only Son . . ." Jesus said in John 15:13: "Greater *love* has no one than this, that one *lay down* his life for his friends." Titus 3:4-5 says: "But when the kindness of God our Savior and His *love* for mankind appeared, He *saved us*, not on the basis of deeds which we have done in righteousness, but *according to His mercy*, by the washing of regeneration and renewing by the Holy Spirit."

God's love for us is not based on His emotions, but is demonstrated by His actions. As we grow in our understanding of His love and mercy toward us, we will increasingly desire to demonstrate our love for Him and others actively and in obedience to these commands:

> *You shall love the Lord your God with all your heart, and with all your soul, and with all your mind.*
> *This is the great and foremost commandment.*
> *And a second is like it, You shall love your neighbor as yourself.*
> *On these two commandments depend the whole Law and the Prophets.*
>
> Matt. 22:37-40

Perhaps the best way we can measure our growth in the area of love is to examine what Paul wrote to the Corinthian believers on this subject:

> *Love is patient, love is kind, and is not jealous; love does not brag and is not arrogant,*
> *(love) does not act unbecomingly; it does not seek its own, is not provoked, does not take into account a wrong suffered,*
> *does not rejoice in unrighteousness, but rejoices with the truth;*

(love) bears all things, believes all things, hopes all things, endures all things.
Love never fails . . . .
But now abide faith, hope, love, these three; but the greatest of these is love.

1 Cor. 13:4-8, 13

■ Complete the following statement:
• *Love is...*

■ List some ways people normally express love:

■ What does it mean to *love your neighbor as yourself?*

• How are you expressing love for others?

• For yourself?

■ What do you think it means to *love the Lord your God with all your heart, soul and mind?*

■ How are you expressing love for God...
- with your heart?

- with your mind?

- with your soul?

■ How has Christ demonstrated His love for you?

■ How does experiencing His love help you to love others?

■ Contrast the effects of love and criticism:
- Love:

- Criticism:

Sexual Behavior

There is yet another area we must examine before concluding our moral inventory: our sexual behavior.

God, our Creator, fashioned every part of our bodies, including our nerve impulses and sexual responses (Ps. 119:73; 139:13). Our sexuality is His gift to us, ordained by Him for procreation (reproduction) and for our good pleasure. Pleasure, as C.S. Lewis once observed, is God's invention, not Satan's.[4]

Concerning procreation, God wanted to ensure that we would be compelled to preserve the human race by "bearing fruit and multiplying." If this was His intent, many of us will agree that He did a good job, given the seemingly overpowering sexual urges we all experience from time to time.

But why pleasure? We have only to look at the surroundings He provided Adam and Eve in Eden to understand that God's original intent for man included his enjoyment of the earth and all it contained (Gen. 2:8-17). It was Adam, remember, who distorted this plan by rebelling against God. As his descendants, we continue to bear the consequences of Adam's original sin. Despite this, God fully intends for us to enjoy sexual pleasure within the constraints of the marital union, and this for at least three reasons:

• *The pleasure of the sexual union serves as a reminder of the exquisite joy we will experience when we, as believers (called His "bride"), will be joined together with Him, "the bridegroom"* (see Matt. 9:14-15; 25:1-3; John 3:28-29; Rev. 19:7). The marital union itself was created as a symbol of our intimate relationship with God. Our union with Him is one which He has promised will never be broken, regardless of our behavior. To those who receive Him as Lord, He is faithful (see Deut. 7:9).

• *Because God made us, He knows the conditions under which we will be at our best.* He created our sexuality for the safe, trusting confines of marriage, not for promiscuity. When we rebel and pervert this plan, we bring upon ourselves devastating consequences: a negative self-image; the pain of a broken relationship and sometimes, a broken home; marital distrust; shattered lives; distorted perceptions about sex and members of the opposite sex; and in some cases, even death.

• *Sex is ordained for marriage for the sake of children.* If adult lives are shattered by sexual misconduct, what about its impact on children? Some children, victims of rape, incest or a broken parental relationship, carry emotional scars into adulthood that haunt them all their lives. Sometimes these scars are borne out in compulsive behaviors like eating disorders, physical abuse, excessive masturbation, alcoholism, drug and/or sexual addiction. (Some also suffer from a loss of sexual function or desire, and some develop a same-sex sexual orientation as a result of these traumas.)

Sexual sin is manifested in many ways: premarital sex, adultery, homosexuality, pornography, exhibitionism, voyeurism, fetishism, pedophilia, sadism, masochism, incest and necrophilia, among others.

The scope of this book is not such that we can address these issues in detail. Nor do we wish to further burden our readers with added guilt and shame. We condemn sexual deviation; we do not condemn those who, like us, fall into sin. Nor does God (Rom. 8:1).

The point is this: We may have been involved in one or more sexual sins before our addiction, but our eating-disordered thinking and behavior may have carried over into compulsive sexual behavior. Or, we may have experienced nothing but an intense hatred of sex, fueled by misgivings about our sexual identity, about being known intimately by another person, about being touched or about the opposite sex.

Whatever our behavior, we need to examine this area of our lives and draw it out into God's light and love and experience reconciliation with Him through His loving acceptance, mercy and forgiveness.

■ What are some ways our culture distorts our God-given sexuality?

■ Explain any problems you have experienced with your sexuality:

■ If you have misused your sexuality in any of the ways already mentioned, how has this harmed others? Be specific:

Person (first name only)   **Results**

■ How has sexual sin harmed you?

• Has it affected your self-esteem? If so, how?

■ Read 1 Cor. 6:9-20. What does God desire for this area of your life?

■ Are you taking any steps to fulfill His desire for you? If so, what are they?

• If not, why are you withholding this area of your life from Him?

• What do you need to enable you to surrender your sexuality to God?

For Additional Reflection and Application

Step 4 has given us an opportunity to put courage into practice. Looking at ourselves is usually scary, but by it we learn what is good and needs to be retained, and what we need to submit to God for change and healing.

We will need to hang onto our courage and ask God for more as we continue forward. For now, however, we need to think about and enjoy the freedom we've experienced by bringing into the light those things we feared about ourselves, ending their reign over our lives.

In his essay, " 'Miserable Offenders,' " C.S. Lewis discusses the benefits of a self-inventory, and writes:

> ... *I think that this steady facing of what one does know* (about oneself) *and bringing it before God, without excuses, and seriously asking for Forgiveness and Grace, and resolving as far as in one lies to do better, is the only way in which we can ever begin to know the fatal thing* (about ourselves) *which is always there . . . preventing us from becoming perfectly just to our wife or husband, or being a better employer or employee . . . .*
>
> *Does that sound very gloomy? Does Christianity encourage morbid introspection? The alternative is much more morbid. Those who do not think of their own sins make up for it by thinking incessantly about the sins of others. It is healthier to think of one's own. It is the reverse of morbid. It is not even, in the long run, very gloomy. A serious attempt to repent and really know one's own sins is in the long run a lightening and relieving process. Of course, there is bound to be a first dismay and often terror and later great pain, yet that is much less in the long run than the anguish of a mass of unrepented and unexamined sins, lurking in the background of our minds. It is the difference between the pain of the tooth about which you should go to the dentist, and the simple straight-forward pain which you know is getting less and less every moment when you have had the tooth out.*[5]

Step Five
My Freedom Through Confession

**We admit to God, to ourselves and to
another person the exact nature
of our wrongs.**

*Therefore, confess your sins to one another, and
pray for one another, so that you may be healed.*
James 5:16a

Once upon a time, a group of clergymen got together for some serious soul-searching and sharing, their goal an experience that would bring them closer together. It was an ecumenical gathering, with all denominations and sects represented from throughout their city. In the spirit of fellowship that prevailed, it was decided that these men of God, behind closed doors, would unburden themselves by confessing to each other the ghastly sins that plagued them most.

There was much shuffling of feet, until one brother arose and confessed that he struggled with sexual lust. Another, inspired by the courage of the first, rose to his feet and announced that he struggled with envy. Still another then summoned his courage and stated that he once had embezzled his church's benevolence fund.

Throughout the evening, these men of God humbled themselves, each in turn, and shared with the group his "secret sin." When they finally reached the last pastor, he arose and declared, "My pet sin is gossip, and I can't wait to get out of here!"

Most of us try to keep our "secret sins" hidden because we lack trust in others and fear that any disclosure will fall into the hands of someone with "loose lips," or someone who will exploit the information about us to harm us, like the clergyman in the story above. In fact, when completing the content of step 4, we may have experienced a sudden urge to protect our twelve-step workbook! This is why we have a unique and difficult struggle with step 5. Most of us were able to confess our sins to God, but once we have confessed to God, why, we wonder, do we have to tell another person?

At least three factors explain to us why this is necessary: the *Forgiveness Factor*, the *Freedom Factor* and the *Fellowship Factor*.

109

The Forgiveness Factor

Most of us have difficulty with realizing and owning God's forgiveness for two basic reasons: (1) We cannot forgive ourselves; (2) We cannot forgive others. But we desperately need to experience forgiveness because it is our deep-seated feelings of shame that fuel our eating disorder and its accompanying behaviors. When we bring our hidden guilt and shame into the open with a sponsor, clergyman, counselor, doctor—someone who has demonstrated that he or she can be trusted—we somehow find it easier to receive forgiveness and experience freedom from the burden of our sins. In the traditional "Order for Holy Communion" of the *Book of Common Prayer,* the "General Confession" includes these words:

> *. . . And are heartily sorry for these our misdoings;*
> *The remembrance of them is grievous unto us;*
> *The burden of them is intolerable.[1]*

Whether or not we actually *experience* our "misdoings" as "intolerable burdens" all the time, they do burden us intolerably by necessitating our eating-disordered behavior. We must literally unburden ourselves by confessing our sins to another person and come into the experience of the "Forgiveness Factor."

The Freedom Factor

Once we have experienced forgiveness by receiving it from another person, we also receive freedom for a very important task: forgiving others. If we are truly honest with ourselves, we come to realize that failing to forgive others results from believing that we are morally superior to them— that as victims, we have the right to go on accusing, despising and vilifying them. This is known as "self-righteous indignation," a sinful attitude which separates us from the loving fellowship God intends for us to have with others. Confessing to another person and receiving his or her forgiveness teaches us to be loving and forgiving of others in a practical, positive way. Once we have brought reality to bear on the fiction of our moral superiority, we gain the humility needed to exercise grace and forgiveness to others.

■ Paraphrase the following:

*You have heard that it was said, "Love your neighbor
and hate your enemy."*
    *But I tell you: Love your enemies and pray for those
who persecute you,*
    that you may be sons of your Father in heaven . . . .
    *Be perfect, therefore, as your heavenly Father is
perfect.*

Matt. 5:43-45, 48, NIV

• Paraphrase:

• What does this passage say about true perfection, as opposed to perfect performance, body weight or "self-righteous indignation"?

The Fellowship Factor

Isolation is both a cause and result of compulsive behavior. Addiction thrives on secrecy and aloneness. We avoid getting involved with others because we feel inferior to them or because we fear that they will hurt us. To compensate for these painful feelings, we turn to our food obsession for comfort. Our obsessive behavior breeds anxiety about the possibility of being discovered by others. Our anxiety then propels us further into the addiction. As a result, we feel the intense pain that accompanies loneliness and isolation, and have the compelling and unshakable conviction that we not only are alone in our struggle, but are odd, different and unique in every bad way.

Something surprising happens when we disclose our negative selves to another human being: We learn that unacceptable patterns of behavior do not make us unacceptable people. In addition, we learn that we are not so odd or different or unique, after all! This is especially true if we summon the courage to share parts of our moral inventory to a therapy or support group. Surprisingly, the thing we feared so much—disclosing what we considered to be our sheer awfulness—becomes the vehicle needed to end our desperate, aching loneliness and isolation. When we disclose ourselves to others and allow them to do the same with us, we give heed to Paul's exhortation:

> *Brothers, if someone is caught in a sin, you who are spiritual should restore him gently. But watch yourself, or you may also be tempted.*
> *Carry each other's burdens, and in this way you will fulfill the law of Christ.*
>
> Gal. 6:1-2, NIV

The Fellowship Factor, in particular, is a vehicle of change and healing, because it completely contradicts our old eating-disordered patterns of secret shame, secret compulsion and isolation.

Preparation for Step 5

Before going any further, it is important to understand that our confession does not make us forgiven. We are forgiven because Christ died to pay for our sins. Confession is a means for us to experience our forgiveness, not obtain it.

Confession should be done with an attitude of repentance. Repentance is not a matter of feeling sorry for ourselves because we've been caught. It is turning away from sin and turning instead to God.

Let's look at what happened to one of God's mightiest men when he turned to God under the weight of unconfessed sin:

David: Man After God's Heart

David, the shepherd, psalmist and King of Israel, was called by God "a man after My own heart." But like all of us, David sinned often and greatly. He committed adultery, and then to cover that sin, committed murder! (See 2 Samuel 11.) What made David a man after God's heart was his attitude. He not only was remorseful about his sin, but he confessed it and then repented. Let's look at the process of David's reconciliation to God in Psalm 32:

■ Read verses 1-2.
  • What word does David use to describe the one whose sin is forgiven?

  • What does that mean?

■ Read verses 3-4.

- What happened to David's body when he kept silent about his sin?

- Have you seen any of these effects in your own life? If so, explain:

■ Read verse 5.
  - What did David do about his sin?

  - What was God's response?

■ Read verses 6-7.
  - What does David encourage us to do about our circumstances?

  - What benefits of knowing God does David describe in the above passage?

The latter part of this passage is God's response to David.

■ Read verses 8-11.
  - Understanding the righteous to be those who trust in God, and the wicked to be those who refuse to trust in Him, what does God say will surround...
    - the righteous?

    - the wicked?

  - Whom does God warn us not to be like, and why?

  - What does God promise to do for us when we are reconciled to Him?

- What heart attitudes does God promise we will have when we are responsive to Him?

Dealing with Sin: The Holy Spirit

Before we make confession, we also need to know something about the Holy Spirit's work of showing us our sins.

As believers, we have received the Spirit of Christ within us. This exercise will help you understand the ministry of the Holy Spirit as He convicts us of sin and guides us into truth. You also will gain insights into confession of sin.

■ Read John 14:16-17. Why do you need a Helper? (2 1/2 lns)

■ What do the following passages say about the role of the Holy Spirit in teaching truth to you?

- John 14:26

- John 16:13

- 1 Cor. 2:11-13

■ Read 2 Tim. 3:16-17. How does the Holy Spirit use Scripture in our lives?

■ Another role of the Holy Spirit is to convict the world concerning sin, righteousness and judgment (John 16:8-11).

- What does it mean to be *convicted*?

- What is the purpose of the Holy Spirit's conviction?

■ Read 1 John 1:9.

- What is *confession*?

• Does confession make you forgiven?

The Lord Jesus realized that once He left the world, His followers would need help. The Holy Spirit, our helper and teacher, was sent to dwell within believers and to be our source of wisdom and strength. The Holy Spirit helps us to live in a way that honors Christ by convicting us of our ungodliness. Conviction allows us to deal with sin in our lives so that we can continue to experience God's love, power and wisdom.

You may be preparing to confess your sins to God for the first time ever. If you need some help, you might use the following as a guide:

> *Dear Father,*
>
> *The Holy Spirit has shown me that I sinned when I* (name sins of thoughts and actions as specifically as possible). *Thank You that I am completely forgiven, and that You choose not to remember my sins. I realize that You have declared me to be deeply loved, completely forgiven, fully pleasing, totally accepted and a new creature—complete in Christ. Amen.*

Some additional insights into confession will be beneficial to us as we move forward in our walk with God:

■ *All sin is against God.*

In Ps. 51:4, we find another account of David as he confessed his sin of adultery and murder before God:

> *Against Thee, Thee only, I have sinned, and done what*
> *is evil in Thy sight, so that Thou art justified when Thou*
> *dost speak, and blameless when Thou dost judge.*

Although others had been affected by his sin, David recognized that its commission was primarily against God. In confronting David, Nathan the prophet asked, "Why have you despised the word of the Lord by doing evil in His sight?" (2 Sam. 12:9). Notice that the focus is on God, not David or others.

From this we realize that when we have the truth of God's Word to guide us, and still choose to sin, God says we are despising Him. Perhaps if before choosing to sin, we would say to God, "I despise You and Your Word," we would be more aware of how sin grieves our heavenly Father.

■ *Confession recognizes the full scope of sin.*

Correct confession requires us to recognize that not only is a specific act sinful, but that the ungodly thoughts and false beliefs which generated our ungodliness are sinful as well. The excuses we might use to justify our sins are part of the ungodly thoughts that cause us to act in a sinful manner. When dealing with sin, we must deal with the root of our actions.

■ *Confession involves accepting our forgiveness in Christ.*

All too often, Christians construct a penance cycle that they believe they must put themselves through before they can feel forgiven. Once convicted of a sin, they might plead with God for forgiveness, and then feel depressed for a couple of days just to show that they really are sorry and deserve to be forgiven.

The truth is that Jesus Christ died on the cross for our sins and has declared us justified by that deed. God not only forgives, He also forgets. Hebrews 10:17 says, . . . *their sins and their lawless deeds I will remember no more.*

We cannot earn forgiveness by punishing ourselves. Confession is simply an application of the forgiveness we already have in Christ. Accepting our forgiveness allows us to move on in our fellowship with the Lord and serve Him joyfully.

■ *True confession involves repentance.*

Repentance means turning away from sin and turning instead to God. When we truly repent, we have a change of attitude about sin. In fact, because repentance involves recognizing the gravity of our sin, it should grieve us as much as it does God.

■ *True confession may involve restitution.*

In confession, it may be necessary to right a wrong. You may need to go to a specific person you have wronged and ask for his or her forgiveness, return something that you stole or fix or replace something that you damaged. Step 5 is preparation for our restitution in steps 8 and 9.

Finally, as we come before God to confess our sins, it should be with the knowledge (or reminder) that our Savior and Lord, Jesus Christ, was tempted in all areas of life, just as we are. There is no temptation experienced by man that Jesus didn't also experience. The writer of Hebrews tells us:

Therefore, He had to be made like His brethren in all things, that He might become a merciful and faithful high priest in things pertaining to God, to make propitiation for the sins of the people.

For since He Himself was tempted in that which He has suffered, He is able to come to the aid of those who are tempted.

Heb. 2:17-18

For we do not have a high priest who cannot sympathize with our weaknesses, but one who has been tempted in all things as we are, yet without sin.

Let us therefore draw near with confidence to the throne of grace, that we may receive mercy and may find grace to help in time of need.

Heb. 4:15-16

• What confidence do these passages give you as you prepare to draw near to His throne?

Choosing a Good Listener

With a better understanding of what it means to confess our wrongs to God, we are ready to analyze the best way to complete a successful fifth step. We begin by determining who will be the best person for us to talk with. Choosing a good listener, choosing the *right* listener is imperative for a good fifth step. In fact, this choice should be made only after prayerful consideration.

The following may be of help to you in your selection process. We urge you to pray for this person with these guidelines in mind:

■ *Choose someone who has completed several years in recovery, or who at least is familiar with the Twelve Steps, and especially step 5 and the issues involved in eating disorders.* Because of the three factors already noted—forgiveness, freedom and fellowship—and their necessity to recovery, step 5 needs to be seen as a life-or-death errand. It can mean the difference between recovery and returning to eating-disordered behavior. A person who is in a twelve-step program, especially for eating

117

disorders, and who has a respectable amount of time in the program will understand this step's importance for you and your recovery.

■ *Choose someone who can keep a confidence.* The information you are preparing to disclose is very personal. The person you select to talk with should be completely trustworthy in this respect.

■ *Choose an objective listener.* This is not yet the time (it may never be) to talk openly with those who are emotionally involved with us, and who may find that what we have to say is more than they can bear. Be considerate in this respect. Sharing is a responsibility.

■ *Choose someone who may be willing to share personal examples from his or her own life with you.* The person you talk with should be a good listener, but it is often through an exchange that you will find the acceptance you especially need right now.

• List some people who might be good listeners for you:

• How will you choose the person best for you to talk with?

• When will you talk to him or her?

Telling a Story

Once we have found a good listener, we are ready to get on with the telling. We have found that this works best as a story, the story of our lives.

Perhaps the best way to begin is by taking some notes, starting from the very beginning and including those persons, circumstances and events that have affected you most along the way. You will, of course, want to refer back continually to your fourth step to interject all the significant things you have done—positive and negative—over the years.

When you do finally sit down with the person you've chosen—your sponsor, pastor, counselor, physician or trusted friend—you may want to read from your notes or refer back to them as an outline. This is up to you.

The point is to get it ALL out—everything that is significant about your life that has never been said.

We leave you to write your story with some final words of caution: It has been our experience that some people who took the fifth step were disappointed because they experienced no immediate feelings of gratification afterward. A successful fifth step is not determined by feelings, but by disclosing the significant events in your life which need to be shared with another person. We urge you to think on this *before* you take this step so that you can be realistic in your expectations.

Finally, it should be remembered that this step is for *you*. Regardless of whom we choose to share ourselves with, it is imperative to realize that our purpose in taking this step is NOT to please the listener, but to gain healing for ourselves.

Story Outline

■ What was your life like when you were a child? Describe your relationships with your parents, brothers and sisters:

■ Describe how your home life has affected you:

■ When did you first begin your compulsive eating behavior(s)?

■ Go back through the questions listed in step 4, and explain in detail how your eating disorder has affected...

• your self-esteem:

• your relationships with your family:

• your relationships with your friends:

• your job/schoolwork:

- your values:

■ List some of the significant events described in your fourth step:

For Additional Reflection and Application

When we have completed step 5, we discover that we no longer need be hostage to our secret failures and sins. Freed from the tyranny of self-righteous indignation, perfectionism and shame, we can truly agree with the words of Charles Wesley:

> *Long my imprisoned spirit lay,*
> *Fast-bound in sin and nature's night;*
> *Thine Eye diffused a quickening ray—*
> *I woke! My dungeon flamed with light!*
> *My chains fell off, my heart was free—*
> *I rose, went forth, and followed Thee!*
>
> *No condemnation now I dread;*
> *Jesus, and all in Him, is mine.*
> *Alive in Him, my living Head,*
> *And clothed with righteousness Divine.*
> *Bold, I approach the Eternal Throne,*
> *And claim the Crown, through Christ, my own!*[2]

Step Six
My Victorious Surrender

***We commit ourselves to God, desiring that
He remove patterns of sin from our lives.***

*Humble yourselves in the presence of the Lord,
and He will exalt you.*

James 4:10

Many of us with eating disorders share at least one common experience: the perplexity of significant others when we can't "just stop."

"Look, I don't understand . . . Why don't you just stop this goofy stuff? It can't be *that* hard." Indeed, when we tried to stop our behavior in the past, we often asked ourselves the same question. *This really is bizarre behavior; why can't I just make up my mind and knock it off?* Then we discovered in step 1 that we were powerless over our compulsion and needed spiritual help to begin our recovery. Now we come to that place when, after having examined ourselves and confessed our sins, we recognize that we need for God to continue the growth and restoration process by removing, not just our compulsive food behavior, but all of those patterns which govern our sinful behavior.

At first glance, step 6 does not seem to be such a big deal. *Patterns of sin? Okay, God, take 'em away. Gee, that was easy!*

Brace yourself: It ain't that easy! Like all persons with eating disorders, we have grown accustomed to a way of thinking which stresses relief from pain over genuine change. In fact, most people seek help to get rid of pain, not to make great changes in their personalities or ways of relating to others.

If we are truly honest with ourselves, we realize that we have long-established patterns of sinful behavior in our lives because we have gotten a lot of mileage out of them. We hang on to them because they give us nice pay-offs, and those pay-offs have become mighty important to us. People-pleasing means we need not risk confronting others with the truth; we can just be "nice" and avoid the unpleasantness that often accompanies confrontation (never mind that the truth takes a beating in the meantime). Perfectionism often receives a lot of positive reinforcement in the workplace;

131

never mind that it can drive us to self-murder as we relentlessly pursue the "perfect" body weight or size. In pursuit of perfection, we also may blame others for past hurts and thereby feel superior to them. Many of us have learned to lie and steal and cloak ourselves in secrecy to maintain our sense of control, and now the truth is often slippery in our grasp—even about things that have nothing to do with our eating behavior. It may be easier—perhaps effortless—to lie than to tell the truth; to shoplift instead of pay, even when we have the money; to withdraw and hide ourselves from others instead of interact with them. These patterns of sin and others are now as impossible for us to conquer by our willpower as was our eating disorder.

Despite this truth, we must avoid falling into the trap of believing, *I am what I am. I cannot change. My situation is hopeless.* God not only has promised us freedom, healing and eternal life, but has promised us changed lives through regeneration. Such is the goal of step 6: Placing our lives in His hands and willingly agreeing that His ways are right, we allow Him to remove our self-destructive patterns of behavior.

This is not a one-time, presto-change-o event. Our compulsive nature wants "the big fix" and wants it *NOW!* We need to understand that although our regeneration in Christ was accomplished at the moment of our conversion, it is reaffirmed in our experience of living one day at a time, with each new day a new beginning. We want to "be there," to have "arrived." We want the pay-off, the finish line. We are far more interested in receiving the Olympic gold than in completing the 100-meter run. God is interested in our *journey*, in *how* we run the course. Even more important to Him, however, is the *runner*, not the *race*. As we run, we grow and mature. And as we run, God perfects us in Him. But the course of the race itself is a lifetime journey. Step 6, then, is not just a step along the way, but a commitment to a new way of life.

One of the obstacles to making this commitment is that although we may be Christians, we still may be uncertain that God is capable of transforming our lives. We lack faith in His resurrection power. In addition, we may feel that we are unworthy of His love, which can so drastically change our lives. We also may have misperceptions about the true character of God. These can lead to wrong motives in serving Him and seeking Him as our source of healing. Finally, we may be trying to achieve spiritual growth through our own determination and willpower, rather than relying on the Holy Spirit, His instrument of change.

Let's examine each of these to discover where we are now in our relationship with God.

Lack of Faith

■ Read the eleventh chapter of Hebrews.
  • From this chapter, give a brief definition of faith:

  • What account of faith given here impresses you most, and why?

  • To what area of your life can you apply this example of faith? Be specific.

■ Read Rom. 10:8-17. What do you learn from this passage about acquiring faith?

■ Read Phil. 2:9-11; Col. 1:15-20; Heb. 2:14-15; 4:15. From these passages, give some reasons why we can depend on Jesus Christ as our source of strength and obedience:

  • How can His authority and power over evil help you to resist temptation and stand firm in obedience?

■ Read Is. 7:7, 9 and Eph. 6:10-18.
  • Why is faith so important in our battle against evil?

  • How does a shield protect the warrior in battle?

  • In what practical ways can you *take up the shield of faith* in your life?

■ Read Luke 11:5-13 with Luke 18:1-8.
- How do the man's persistence in Luke 11 and the woman's persistence in Luke 18 prove their faith?

- How do *asking, seeking* and *knocking* demonstrate faith?

- What are the strengths and weaknesses of your relationship with God at this point in your life?
  . . . Strengths:

  . . . Weaknesses:

- In what areas of your life do you need to be more persistent (or faithful)?

- What factors would help you both to persist and to grow in your relationship with God? (Consider supportive relationships, honesty, the Scriptures, the Holy Spirit, specific choices and habits, time).

Feelings of Unworthiness
■ Read Luke 7:36-48, 50.
- If we liken the Pharisee in this passage to our society today, what is the difference between the Lord's view of sinners and society's view?

- Do you think Jesus finds it harder to forgive "big sins" than "little sins"?

- This woman's heart was filled with gratitude toward Jesus in response to His love for her. She demonstrated her gratitude in action. In what practical ways can you demonstrate your gratitude to the Lord Jesus in your daily life?

Misunderstanding the True Character of God

The following is a list of attitudes about God and relating to Him that are shared by many people who have eating disorders.[1]

- *God is mean.* Many of us don't truly believe that God has our best interests at heart. Perhaps we have seen others reap God's blessings in tangible ways, while nothing good seems to be happening in our own lives. We may have thus concluded that God loves others, but only wants to punish us.

  Some of us believe that God wants to rob us rather than enrich us. This is one of Satan's ploys. When he appeared to Eve in the Garden of Eden, he didn't say, "Wow! Look at all these trees from which you can eat! God certainly has blessed you!" Instead, he focused her attention on the one tree that was forbidden to her (see Gen. 3:5-6). He does the same with us today by drawing our attention to the restrictions rather than the blessings of Christian living.[2]
- *The Lord demands too much of me.* A primary reason why people resort to their "compulsion of choice" is to escape responsibility. The basic needs and demands of life seem frightening when we don't have a box of cookies or a set of scales handy. Add to our daily responsibilities the burden of obedience, and many of us may feel overwhelmed.
- *I don't want to lose control of my life.* Those who are dependent are often slow to grasp the truth about "control." Although we can see improvements in our lives as a result of relinquishing that which we thought was enabling us to be in control—our compulsive eating behavior—we can't seem to transfer this concept to other areas of our lives. We may even be willing to admit that we gained control over our lives when we stopped our eating-disordered behavior. Yet we continue to hedge on allowing Christ to rule our lives, still unable to grasp that His lordship is our ticket to freedom.
- *I don't want to be perceived as weird.* Many of us have been isolated from true intimacy and companionship by the numbing, excluding aspects of our eating disorder. Some of us still haven't developed friendships with others because we have long-established habits of hiding and secrecy, which were characteristic of our eating disorder.

135

When we add to these circumstances our feelings of aloneness as recovering dependents, we may also feel terrified of how others will respond if we take a stand for Christ in our daily affairs.

■ Which of the above attitudes do you see in your own life? What causes you to feel this way?

■ It is important to understand that all of these attitudes are misperceptions. Take a moment now to tell God how you are feeling by putting your thoughts in writing. Then ask Him to convey His truth to you as you have opportunities to trust Him in the months ahead.

Examining the Truth

In the exercise below, we will examine some truths about God.
■ Read John 1:17-18; 14:8-10. How can you know the truth about God's character?

■ Christ perfectly reveals the Father to us. What does each of these passages teach you about Christ?
• John 4:13-18, 39

• John 10:15

• John 14:2-3

- John 15:13-15

- John 17:23

■ Using the content of the previous passages of Scripture, write a few sentences explaining how God relates to you and feels about you.
I know that my heavenly Father . . .

■ Read Psalm 103. In the left column, write characteristics of God the Father that you see in this psalm. In the right column, write out what difference this characteristic makes in your life.
My heavenly Father is . . .   As a result I . . .

It is critical that we accurately know the one true God. We will only follow someone whom we know and trust. Satan deceives us by distorting the character of God: *If you follow and obey God, you'll be miserable. God doesn't love you because you did this. God won't accept someone like you.* By deceiving us about God's love and power, Satan robs us of the desire to love, obey and honor Him.

How can we overcome the subtle deceptions of the enemy? Paul wrote that we are to be transformed by the renewing of our minds (Rom. 12:2), but we cannot combat the *spiritual forces of wickedness* (Eph. 6:12) with our own human resources. Nor can we experience transformation in accordance with God's will through intellectual enlightenment or the power of positive thinking. Scripture says: *You are from God, little children, and have overcome them* [demonic forces]; *because greater is He who is in you than he who is in the world* (1 John 4:4). The work of our transformation is God's, and He accomplishes that work through the One who comes to reside within us at the moment of our spiritual birth: the Holy Spirit.

The Holy Spirit

The Holy Spirit, the third Person of the Trinity, is God and possesses all the attributes of deity. His primary purpose is to glorify Christ and bring attention to Him. Christ said, *He shall glorify Me; for He shall take of mine, and shall disclose it to you* (John 16:14). The Holy Spirit is our teacher, and He guides us into the truth of the Scriptures (John 16:13). It is by His power that the love of Christ flows through us and produces spiritual fruit within us (John 7:37-39; 15:1-8).

In Gal. 5:22, this spiritual fruit is described as *love, joy, peace, patience, kindness, goodness, faithfulness, gentleness, self-control.* In other passages in the New Testament, it is described as *intimate friendship with Christ* (John 15:14), *love for one another* (John 15:12), *joy and peace in the midst of difficulties* (John 14:27; 15:11), *steadfastness* (1 Cor. 15:58), *singing, thankfulness and submission* (Eph. 5:18-21) and *evangelism and discipleship* (Matt. 28:18-20).

Reading this, we initially may feel dismayed, realizing that many of these qualities are absent from our lives—whether we've known the Lord for a long time or not.

We must remember that Christianity is not a self-improvement program and that our goal is not perfection. When perfection is our aim, we become prideful and motivated to perform by rules. This is not God's intent, nor should it be ours. Our goal is to *mature* in Christ until the day we shall be glorified with Him and become like Him (1 John 3:2). We grow toward maturity as we draw on Christ for direction, encouragement and strength.

To better understand this, let's look at what Jesus said in John 15:1, 4-5:

> *I am the true vine, and My Father is the vine dresser.*
> *. . . Abide in* (live, grow, and gain your sustenance from) *Me, and I in you. As the branch cannot bear fruit of itself, unless it abides in the vine, so neither can you, unless you abide in Me.*
> *I am the vine, you are the branches; he who abides in Me, and I in him, he bears much fruit; for apart from Me you can do nothing.*

Nothing? Yes, in terms of that which is honoring to Christ, is spiritually nourishing to us and is genuinely Christian service, anything done apart from the love and power of Christ amounts to nothing. Although we may expend tremendous effort at great personal cost, only that which is done for Christ's glory in the power of His Spirit is of eternal value. The very power of God that was evident when Christ was raised from the dead (Eph. 1:19-

21) is available to every believer who abides in Him, who desires to honor Him and who trusts that His Spirit will produce fruit in his or her life.

The Battle Within

To experience the Holy Spirit's power in our lives we first must understand that as Christians, a continual battle is working within us. Each time we move toward the cross to do those things that are pleasing to God, our "flesh," or human nature, compels us to retreat. On the other hand, when we begin to venture toward sin, the Holy Spirit prompts us to obey.

> *But I say, walk by the Spirit, and you will not carry out the desire of the flesh.*
> *For the flesh sets its desires against the Spirit, and the Spirit against the flesh; for these are in opposition to one another, so that you may not do the things that you please.*
> Gal. 5:16-17

> *For I know that nothing good dwells in me, that is, in my flesh; for the wishing is present in me, but the doing of the good is not.*
> *For the good that I wish, I do not do; but I practice the very evil that I do not wish.*
> *I find then the principle that evil is present in me, the one who wishes to do good.*
> *For I joyfully concur with the law of God in the inner man,*
> *but I see a different law in the members of my body, waging war against the law of my mind, and making me a prisoner of the law of sin which is in my members.*
> Rom. 7:18-19, 21-23

In addition to this struggle we face against our own flesh, we also are in a continual battle as God's elect against Satan and his unseen forces. As Paul wrote to the believers in Ephesus:

> *For our struggle is not against flesh and blood, but against the rulers, against the powers, against the world forces of this darkness, against the spiritual forces of wickedness in the heavenly places.*
> Eph. 6:12

The only way we can hope to achieve victory over these struggles is through the power of the Holy Spirit.

The following exercise will help you understand how God can empower you to live according to His truth by depending on His Spirit to complete the work He has started within you (Phil. 1:6).

■ Read John 7:37-39 and answer the following questions:
- *If any man is thirsty* is a metaphor for our desire and need for Christ. What does it mean to *drink* of Christ?

- In what ways are you *thirsty* for Him?

- What are some aspects of the Christian life that *rivers of living water* might symbolize?

- Jesus said that these "rivers" flow from our *innermost being*. What does this mean to you?

■ Read John 15:1-8. This passage contains another metaphor which illustrates that the Holy Spirit is the source of a life that honors Christ. Answer the following:

- Describe how a branch produces fruit (vv. 4-5):

- What are some evidences of spiritual *fruit* within the believer's life?

- John 15:2 says that God prunes every fruitful branch, that it may bear more fruit. Can you think of some ways God might *prune* us?

• What are some things that prevent a branch from producing fruit?

• What could prevent you from living a more fruitful, Christ-honoring life?

• Summarize Christ's teaching in these two passages (John 7:37-39; 15:1-8) in your own words:

We can't accomplish God's will by self-effort. The Holy Spirit gives us the wisdom and the strength to turn from sin and walk with God in obedience. At the same time, God doesn't act alone. We experience His victory as we cooperate with Him. Our part is to be responsive and responsible. His part is to work in and through us as Paul wrote the Colossians: *And for this purpose also I labor, striving according to His power which mightily works within me* (Col. 1:19).

In the following exercise, we will examine six biblical motives for choosing to cooperate with God by acting in obedience, rather than choosing to live in sin and self-effort.

Motivations for Obedience

God's love and acceptance of us are based on His grace, His unmerited favor, not on our ability to impress Him through our good deeds. If we are accepted on the basis of His grace and not our deeds, why should we obey God? According to scriptural principles, there are at least six proper motivations for obedience:

Christ's Love
When we experience love, we usually respond by seeking to express our love in return. Our obedience to God is an expression of our love for Him (John 14:15, 21), which comes from an understanding of what Christ has

accomplished for us on the cross (2 Cor. 5:14-15). We love because He first loved us and clearly demonstrated His love for us at the cross (1 John 4:16-19). This great motivating factor is missing in many of our lives because we don't really believe that God loves us unconditionally. We expect His love to be conditional, based on our ability to earn it.

Our experience of God's love is based on our perception. If we believe that He is demanding or aloof, we will not experience His love and tenderness. Instead, we either will be afraid of Him or angry with Him. Faulty perceptions of God often prompt us to rebel against Him.

Our image of God is the foundation for all of our motivations. As we grow in our understanding of His unconditional love and acceptance, we will increasingly want our lives to bring honor to the One who loves us so much.

■ Does the love of Christ compel you to obey Him? Why or why not?

Sin Is Destructive

Satan has effectively blinded man to the painful, damaging consequences of sin. The effects of sin are all around us, yet many continue to indulge in the pleasure-seeking and rampant self-centeredness that cause so much anguish and pain. Satan contradicted God in the Garden when he said, *You surely shall not die!* (Gen. 3:4). Sin is pleasant, but only for a season. Sooner or later, it will result in some form of destruction.

Sin is destructive in many ways. Emotionally, we can experience guilt and shame as well as the fears of failure and punishment. Mentally, we may experience painful flashbacks and expend enormous amounts of time and energy thinking about our sins and rationalizing our guilt. Physically, we may suffer psychosomatic disorders or a number of other complications (some of which may result from our eating disorder). Relationally, we can alienate ourselves from others. Spiritually, we grieve the Holy Spirit, lose our testimony and break our fellowship with God. The painful and destructive effects of sin are so profound that why we don't have an aversion to it is a mystery!

■ Read the first chapter of Jonah. List the results of Jonah's choice of disobedience to God:

■ In what ways have you seen specific effects of a particular sin in your life?

■ How can viewing sin as destructive be a motivation for being obedient to God?

Satan is a master of deception and subtlety. He whispers promising suggestions to us. When these thoughts first enter the mind, they hint only at the possibility of forthcoming pleasure, not devastating consequences. While God does allow us to be tempted—something we have no control over—He has given us His Word and His Spirit so that we can resist Satan and live in obedience to Him.

■ Read James 4:7-8 and 1 John 4:4. What comforts do you receive from these passages?

■ What are some ways you can resist Satan's attacks of temptation in the future?

The Father's Discipline

Another purpose of the Holy Spirit is to convict us of sin. Conviction is a form of God's discipline, which serves as proof that we have become sons of God (Heb. 12:5-11). It warns us that we are making choices without regard to either God's truth or sin's consequences. If we choose to be unresponsive to the Holy Spirit, our heavenly Father will discipline us in love. Many people do not understand the difference between discipline and punishment. The following chart shows their profound contrasts:

	PUNISHMENT	DISCIPLINE
SOURCE:	God's Wrath	God's Love
PURPOSE:	To Avenge a Wrong	To Correct a Wrong
RELATIONAL RESULT:	Alienation	Reconciliation
PERSONAL RESULT:	Guilt	A Righteous Lifestyle
DIRECTED TOWARD:	Non-Believers	His Children

Jesus bore all the punishment we deserved on the cross. Therefore, we no longer need to fear punishment from God for our sins. We should seek to do what is right so that our Father will not have to correct us through discipline, but when we are disciplined, we can remember that God is correcting us in love. His discipline leads us to righteous performance, a reflection of the righteousness of Christ.

■ Do you sometimes confuse God's correction with punishment? If so, why?

■ How can understanding God's discipline be a motivation for you to obey Him?

God's Commands for Us Are Good

God's commands are given for two good purposes: to protect us from the destructiveness of sin and to direct us in a life of joy and fruitfulness. We have a wrong perspective if we only view God's commands as restrictions in our lives. Instead, we must realize that His commands are guidelines, given so that we might enjoy life to the fullest. In addition, God's commands are holy, right and good. Therefore, since they have value in themselves, we should choose to obey God and follow His commands.

Avoid trying to keep God's commands by legalism and self-effort. That leads only to bitterness, condemnation and rigidity. The Holy Spirit will give you power, joy and creativity as you trust Him to fulfill the commands of God's Word through you.

■ Read Rom. 7:12 and 1 John 5:3. How are God's commands described?

■ Read Deut. 5:29; 6:24. What are some results of obeying God's commands?

■ How can viewing God's commands as good motivate you to obey them?

Our Obedience Will Be Rewarded

Our self-worth is not based on our performance and obedience; however, what we do (or don't do) has tremendous implications on the quality of our lives and our impact on others for Christ's sake. Disobedience results in spiritual poverty; a short-circuiting of intimate fellowship with the One who loves us so much that He died for us; confusion, guilt and frustration; and an absence of spiritual power and desire to see people won to Christ and become disciples. On the other hand, responding to the love, grace and power of Christ enables us to experience His love, joy and strength as we minister to others, endure difficulties and live for Him who has . . . *called us out of darkness into His marvelous light* (1 Pet. 2:9). We are completely loved, forgiven and accepted apart from our performance, but how we live is very important!

■ Read 1 Cor. 3:11-15; 2 Cor. 5:10; 1 John 4:17 and Rev. 20:11-15. According to these passages, those who reject Christ will be judged and condemned at the Great White Throne of Judgment. Though believers will be spared from this condemnation, we will stand before the Judgment Seat of Christ to have our deeds tested. Deeds done for the Lord will be honored, but deeds done for ourselves will be destroyed by fire. The Greek word to describe this judgment seat is the same word used to describe the platform on which an athlete stands to receive his wreath of victory for winning an event. The Judgment Seat is for the reward of good deeds, not for the punishment of sin.

The following chart demonstrates some of the differences between the Judgment Seat of Christ and the Great White Throne Judgment:

	JUDGMENT SEAT OF CHRIST (1 Cor. 3:11-15)	**GREAT WHITE THRONE OF JUDGMENT** (Rev. 20:11)
WHO WILL APPEAR:	Christians	Non-Christians
WHAT WILL BE JUDGED:	Deeds	Deeds
PERSONAL RESULT:	Reward	Condemnation
ULTIMATE RESULT:	Used to honor Christ	Cast out of God's presence into the lake of fire

■ Read 1 Cor. 9:24-27 and 2 Tim. 2:3-7; 4:7-8. How does receiving a reward become a motivation for obedience?

Christ Is Worthy

Our most noble motivation for serving Christ is simply that He is worthy of our love and obedience. The apostle John recorded his vision of the Lord and his response to His glory:

> After these things I looked, and behold, a door standing open in heaven, and the first voice which I had heard, like the sound of a trumpet speaking with me, said, "Come up here, and I will show you what must take place after these things."
>
> Immediately I was in the Spirit; and behold, a throne was standing in heaven, and One sitting on the throne.
>
> And He who was sitting was like a jasper stone and a sardius in appearance; and there was a rainbow around the throne, like an emerald in appearance.
>
> And around the throne were twenty-four thrones; and upon the thrones I saw twenty-four elders sitting, clothed in white garments, and golden crowns on their heads . . .
>
> And when the living creatures give glory and honor and thanks to Him who sits on the throne, to Him who lives forever and ever,
>
> the twenty-four elders will fall down before Him who sits on the throne, and will worship Him who lives forever and ever, and will cast their crowns before the throne, saying,
>
> "Worthy art Thou, our Lord and our God, to receive glory and honor and power; for Thou didst create all things, and because of Thy will they existed, and were created."
>
> Rev. 4:1-4, 9-11

Each time we choose to obey, we express the righteousness we have in Christ. Our performance, then, becomes a reflection of who we are in Him, and we draw on His power and wisdom so that we can honor Him.

■ Read 1 Cor. 3:16-17 and 1 Pet. 2:9. How are you described?

■ What purposes for our lives do these passages suggest?

■ How much are you motivated by each of these six reasons to obey God? Reflect on these motivations and rate each on a scale of zero (no motivation to you at all) to ten (a persistent, conscious, compelling motivation):

_____The love of Christ motivates us to obey Him.
_____Sin is destructive.
_____The Father will discipline us if we continue in a habit of sin.
_____His commands for us are good.
_____We will receive rewards for obedience.
_____Christ is worthy of our obedience.

■ Do any of these seem "purer" or "higher" to you? If so, which ones? Why?

■ Which of these do you need to concentrate on? What can you do to develop this motivation further?

Improper Motivations for Obedience

Jesus repeatedly emphasized that His concern is not only what we do, but why we do it. The Pharisees obeyed many rules and regulations, but their hearts were far from the Lord. Motives are important! The following represent some poor motivations for obeying God and their possible results:

Someone May Find Out

Many people obey God because they are afraid of what others will think of them if they don't obey. Allen went on church visitation because he feared what his Sunday school class would think if he didn't. Barbara was married, but wanted to go out with a man at work. She didn't because of what others might think.

There are problems with determining behavior solely on the opinions of others. First, there are times when no one is watching. If the motive to refrain from sin is missing, we may indulge in it. A second problem is that our desire to disobey may eventually exceed the peer pressure to obey. Finally, once someone has found out we've sinned, we may no longer have a reason to obey.

■ Is the "fear of someone finding out" a motivation for you to obey God? If it is, identify the specific sin you are trying to avoid; then go back over the six reasons to obey Him. Which of these proper motives seems to encourage you most in regard to your specific sin?

God Will Be Angry with Me

Some people obey God because they think He will get angry with them if they don't. We've already discussed the difference in God's discipline and punishment, but to reiterate, God disciplines us in love, not anger. His response to our sin is grief, not condemnation (Eph. 4:30).

Hank was afraid that God would "zap" him if he did anything wrong, so he performed for God. He lived each day in fear of God's anger. Predictably, his relationship with the Lord was cold and mechanical.

God does want our respect, but He doesn't want us to live in fear of His anger. He wants our lives to be a response to His love. This produces joyful obedience instead of fear.

■ If you knew that God's response to your sin was grief instead of anger, would that affect your motivation to obey Him? Why or why not?

I Couldn't Approve of Myself if I Didn't Obey

Some people obey God in an attempt to live up to certain standards they've set for themselves. Sadly, the idea of yielding their lives to a loving Lord is often far from their minds. They only are trying to live up to their own standards, and if they don't meet those standards, they feel ashamed. These people are primarily concerned with do's and don'ts. Instead of an intimate relationship with God, they see the Christian life as a ritual, with the key emphasis on rules. If these people succeed in keeping the rules, they often become prideful. They also may tend to compare themselves with others, hoping to be accepted on the basis of being a little bit better than someone else.

Phillip was raised in a strict church family. He was taught that cursing is a terrible sin. All of Phillip's friends cursed, but he never did. He secretly thought that he was better than his friends. The issue with Phillip was never what God wanted or God's love for him. Instead, it was his own compulsion to live up to his standards. Phillip needed to base his behavior on God and His Word, not on his own standards.

God gave us His commands out of love for us. We are freed to enjoy life more fully as we obey Him.

■ What things are you not doing because you couldn't stand yourself if you did them? What are you doing to obey God with the motivation to meet your own standards?

I'll Obey to Be Blessed

God doesn't swap marbles. If our sole motive to obey is to be blessed, we are simply attempting to manipulate God. The underlying assumption is: *I've been good enough . . . bless me.* It's true that we will reap what we sow. It's true that obedience keeps us within God's plan for us. But our decision to obey never should be based solely on God's rewarding us.

Brian went to church so that God would bless his business, not because he wanted to worship God. Cheryl chose not to spread gossip about Diane because she had told God that she wouldn't tell anybody about Diane if He would get her the promotion she wanted.

Similarly, we may try to bargain with God, saying, *I'll obey You if You will "fix" me.* We reason that if we are "fixed," we will be better equipped to serve God (and we'll be freed from having to deal with a particular problem or temptation). However, God sometimes has something important to teach us through a particular weakness.

The apostle Paul entreated the Lord three times, asking Him to remove a "thorn," or difficulty, from him. The Lord responded to him: *My grace is sufficient for you, for power is perfected in weakness* (2 Cor. 12:9). Paul concluded: *Most gladly, therefore, I will rather boast about my weaknesses, that the power of Christ may dwell in me. Therefore I am well content with weaknesses, with insults, with distresses, with persecutions, with difficulties, for Christ's sake; for when I am weak, then I am strong* (2 Cor. 12:10).

■ Do you try to make deals with God? Why or why not?

■ How can you apply Paul's words to overcoming eating-disordered thinking and behavior?

■ To any other situation?

Christ has freed us from the bondage of sin so that we can respond to Him in obedience. We have discussed six biblical reasons to be involved in good works:

1. The love of Christ motivates us to obey Him.
2. Sin is destructive.
3. The Father will discipline us.
4. His commands for us are good.
5. We will receive rewards.
6. Obedience is an opportunity to honor God.

There are times when our feelings seem to get in the way of our obedience. We may want to indulge in some particular sin, or we may be afraid of failure or what someone might think of us. We may be selfish or maybe just tired. But the Lord never said pleasant emotions were a prerequisite for following Him. He said, *If anyone wishes to come after Me, let him deny himself* (and the right to pleasant emotions), *and take up his cross daily, and follow Me* (Luke 9:23). This doesn't mean we should deny our emotions, whether they are positive or negative. We should express them fully to the Lord, telling Him how we feel, and then act in faith on His Word. But spiritual growth, character development and Christian service should not be held hostage by our emotions. God has given each of us a will and we can choose to honor the Lord in spite of our feelings.

In different situations, we will draw upon different motivations for obedience. Sometimes we will need to be reminded of the destructiveness of sin in order to choose righteousness. At other times we will be overwhelmed by God's love and want to honor Him. Either way, it is our underlying motive which determines if our actions are done to honor God or to make us more acceptable to Him, to others or ourselves.

■ Are your emotions prompting you to postpone obedience in any area(s) of your life? If yes, which one(s)?

■ What steps of action do you need to take to obey the Lord?

For Additional Reflection and Application

As you become more aware of correct motives for obedience and begin to identify improper motivations in your life, you may think, *I've never done anything purely for the Lord in my whole life!* You may feel a sense of pain and remorse for your inappropriate motives. Try not to demean yourself for your past attitudes—they are common to all of us. Instead, realize that you are changing and growing. Over the course of this lifetime process, you will continue to find that life is challenging. As you face (rather than hide from) its challenges, you will begin to feel an increasing sense of confidence. You no longer will agree with the ancient Chinese, who stated the curse, "May you live in interesting times." Rather, you will learn to steadily welcome "interesting" times as opportunities for growth and development through which you can become more like God.

Become like God? Consider this:

> *How great is the love the Father has lavished on us,*
> *that we should be called the children of God! And that is*

what we are! The reason the world does not know us is that it did not know him.

Dear friends, now we are children of God, and what we will be has not yet been made known. But we know that when he (Jesus) appears, we shall be like him, for we shall see him as he is.

Everyone who has this hope in him purifies himself, just as he (Jesus) is pure.

1 John 3:1-3, NIV

Step 6 is another life-or-death issue. Most of us interpret *life-or-death* to mean "death." But here we realize that it really comes down to life. We recognize that our compulsion has robbed us of life, has cheated us from the life that should have been ours. In recovery, we discover the gift of new life.

The thief comes only to steal and kill and destroy; I have come that they may have life, and have it to the full.

John 10:10, NIV

You may be old enough to remember the Jack Benny routine, in which a mugger demands at gunpoint, "Your money or your life!" Benny, whose stock in comedy centered on his supposed avarice and extreme tightness with money, always got a laugh as he stalled and mulled it over, finally exclaiming, "Don't rush me! I'm thinking, I'm thinking!" How well we could identify with this in our compulsion, because we could not bring ourselves to consider what we thought were the horrors of life without our addiction. In recovery, we learn that life is worth living, for God has given us infinite worth and meaningful purpose for an abundant life. In step 7 we will discover some new tools for experiencing the transformation necessary to enjoy that life.

Step Seven
My Surrender on the March

**We humbly ask God to renew our minds so
that our sinful patterns can be transformed
into patterns of life and health
and righteousness.**

*And do not be conformed to this world, but be transformed by
the renewing of your mind, that you may prove what the will
of God is, that which is good and acceptable and perfect.*

Rom. 12:2

Perhaps up to this point, you have been dismayed by our focus on eliminating negative aspects of our personalities and behavior. You may have wondered why we have not instead focused on replacing those negatives with positives.

If you decided to wait humbly and see what would transpire as the Twelve Steps unfolded, here your waiting not only will begin to be rewarded, but you actually will be ahead of the game because you decided to wait humbly in the first place. *Humbly*, as it is used in step 7, is important. Humility is not to be confused with humiliation. *Humiliation* occurs when our pride has been bruised; *humility* can never be humiliated, because humility precludes pride altogether.

It often is difficult for us to see ourselves as having a problem with pride, so it is important to understand what exactly pride is. *Pride* is an inordinate emphasis on one's performance over person—literally, being a "human doing" instead of a "human being." Pride is different from "self-esteem," which is estimating personal worth based on who or whose I am, not on what I do. Pride places us in a terribly insecure frame of mind, for if our worth is based on what we can do, what happens if for some reason we can't? We need to humbly ask God to renew our minds and give us healthy self-esteem (*based not on pride, or on what I do, but on justification, which is what God has done and created in me*). In addition, we need to ask Him to help us live within the positive alternatives to the defects of character that we identified in step 4.

Dishonesty	Honesty
Resentment	Forgiveness
Self-Pity (Dejection)	Gratitude
Impatience and Impulsiveness	Patience
False Pride/False Humility	Humility
Destructive Anger	Constructive Anger
Fear	Trust
Criticism	Love

If we seek God with humility, He is most eager to change our lives by replacing our old nature of self-destruction with His nature of renewal. Let's examine what this process of change might look like.

Codependent Behavioral Patterns

As we mentioned in the *Introduction,* those who struggle with eating disorders are likely to also struggle with codependency, the patterns of thinking and behavior which originate out of dysfunctional family systems, and which emphasize relentless over-responsibility for the problems and behavior of "significant others." Codependency in itself is an addiction, like chemical dependency and an eating disorder. For the codependent, the "drug of choice" is one or more dysfunctional relationships characterized by assuming responsibility for a primary dependent person while repressing his or her own needs (physical, emotional, social or spiritual). The "litany of the codependent" is, "Don't talk, don't trust, don't feel." People with eating disorders frequently exhibit codependent behaviors, using the "litany" as a relentless resolution to avoid facing painful issues. As we renew our minds, the transformation gradually will look something like this:

LITANY OF THE CODEPENDENT
Trust my defenses and accept no one.

DON'T TALK	DON'T TRUST	DON'T FEEL
Censor responses.	Don't allow intimacy.	Don't ever experience fear.
Don't give honest feedback.	Don't verbalize feelings.	Don't ever experience hurt.
Don't give my opinion.	Don't let anyone ever get close.	Don't love anyone—they will only hurt me.

REACT AND BE LIFE'S VICTIM

LITANY OF THE RECOVERING CODEPENDENT
Trust God; accept people.

TALK	TRUST	FEEL
Respond appropriately.	Allow intimacy.	Fear is not "bad"—it will not *harm* me.
Give honest feedback—*honestly*.	Be aware of feelings and allow those I choose to trust/ accept to know them.	Accept the fact that I will at times be *hurt* but not *harmed*. I can learn from my hurt and be okay.
Respect my own opinion—even if others don't accept it.	Appreciate closeness.	Accept love's risks.

ACT AND LIVE

One of the major difficulties in overcoming codependency and other manifestations of our eating disorder is the problem of distorted thinking. Solomon wrote, *As* (a man) *thinks within himself, so he is* (Prov. 23:7). In other words, there is a direct relationship between what we think and how we act. Dysfunctional relationships have provided a fertile environment for confusion and delusion. This step is designed to help us examine our thinking process so that we can make substantive, positive changes in the way we think about God, others and ourselves.

Renewing Our Minds

Since the Fall, man's mind has been darkened (Eph. 4:17-19), and he has chosen to believe the lies of Satan instead of the truths of God's Word. Satan's lies are a direct result of his character:

> . . . *He* (Satan) *was a murderer from the beginning, and does not stand in the truth, because there is no truth in him. Whenever he speaks a lie, he speaks from his own nature; for he is a liar, and the father of lies.*
>
> John 8:44

Satan's goal is to keep our minds unrenewed so that our lives won't be transformed. He does this by establishing fortresses of deception, destructive belief systems that are reinforced over the years by the thoughts, emotions and actions they produce.

Our thoughts usually affect the way we feel, the way we perceive others and ourselves, and ultimately, the way we act. Writing to the Christians in Rome, Paul explained the serious implications of how we think:

> *And do not be conformed to this world, but be transformed by the renewing of your mind, that you may prove what the will of God is, that which is good and acceptable and perfect.*
>
> Rom. 12:2

Although the way we think often affects the way we feel (and thus, the way we act), our thoughts, emotions and behaviors are dependent on each other; none exists in a vacuum. However, because beliefs can play a powerful role in shaping our behavior, we will consider their effect on our lives by using a model adapted from psychologist Albert Ellis's Rational Emotive Therapy. A simple explanation of this approach is:

Situations

⇩

Beliefs ⇨ Thoughts ⇨ Emotions ⇨ Actions

This model conveys the idea that we often interpret the situations we encounter through our beliefs. Some of these interpretations are conscious reflections, but most are based on unconscious assumptions. These beliefs—which have been shaped by our environment, experiences and education—trigger certain thoughts, which in turn stimulate certain emotions, and these emotions usually prompt our actions.

False Beliefs

Given the above, it follows that if what we believe about ourselves is founded on the truth of God's Word, then we are likely to have a positive self-esteem. However, as we mentioned in step 2, Satan has deceived most of mankind by convincing us that:

Our Self-Worth = Performance + Others' Opinions

The four false beliefs we included in that step serve as a summary of the many lies Satan tells us. These beliefs are listed again below. Estimate the percentage which you think indicates how much you live by each belief, from zero to 100 percent:

____% *I must meet certain standards in order to feel good about myself.*
____% *I must have the approval of certain others* (boss, friends, parents) *to feel good about myself. If I don't have their approval, I can't feel good about myself.*
____% *Those who fail are unworthy of love and deserve to be blamed or condemned.*
____% *I am what I am. I cannot change. I am hopeless. In other words, I am the sum total of all my past successes and failures, and I'll never be significantly different.*

The following chart identifies each belief with its consequences, God's specific solution and the increasing freedom we will gain by living out His solution.

157

FALSE BELIEFS	CONSEQUENCES OF FALSE BELIEFS
I must meet certain standards in order to feel good about myself.	The fear of failure; perfectionism; being driven to succeed; manipulating others to achieve success; withdrawing from healthy risks
I must have the approval of certain others to feel good about myself.	The fear of rejection; attempting to please others at any cost; being overly sensitive to criticism; withdrawing from others to avoid disapproval
Those who fail (including myself) are unworthy of love and deserve to be punished.	The fear of punishment; propensity to punish others; blaming self and others for personal failure; withdrawing from God and fellow believers; being driven to avoid punishment
I am what I am. I cannot change. I am hopeless.	Feelings of shame, hopelessness, inferiority; passivity; loss of creativity; isolation, withdrawing from others

GOD'S SPECIFIC SOLUTION	RESULTS OF GOD'S SOLUTION
Because of justification, I am completely forgiven and fully pleasing to God. I no longer have to fear failure.	Increasing freedom from the fear of failure; desire to pursue the right things: Christ and His kingdom; love for Christ
Because of reconciliation, I am totally accepted by God. I no longer have to fear rejection.	Increasing freedom from the fear of rejection; willingness to be open and vulnerable; able to relax around others; willingness to take criticism; desire to please God no matter what others think
Because of propitiation, I am deeply loved by God. I no longer have to fear punishment or punish others.	Increasing freedom from the fear of punishment; patience and kindness toward others; being quick to apply forgiveness; deep love for Christ
Because of regeneration, I have been made brand new, complete in Christ. I no longer need to experience the pain of shame.	Christ-centered self-confidence; joy, courage, peace; desire to know Christ

Let's examine these false beliefs with God's solution for each one:

The Performance Trap

The false belief, *I must meet certain standards in order to feel good about myself*, results in a fear of failure. Take the following test to determine how strongly you are affected by this fear.

Fear of Failure Test
Read the following statements. Look at the top of the test and choose the term which best describes your response. Put the number above that term in the blank beside each statement.

1	2	3	4	5	6	7
Always	Very Often	Often	Sometimes	Seldom	Very Seldom	Never

____ 1. Because of fear, I often avoid participating in certain activities.
____ 2. When I sense I might experience failure in some important area, I become nervous and anxious.
____ 3. I worry.
____ 4. I have unexplained anxiety.
____ 5. I am a perfectionist.
____ 6. I am compelled to justify my mistakes.
____ 7. There are certain areas in which I feel I must succeed.
____ 8. I become depressed when I fail.
____ 9. I become angry with people who interfere with my attempts to succeed, and as a result, make me appear incompetent.
____10. I am self-critical.
_____ Total (Add up the numbers you have placed in the blanks.)

Interpretation of Score
If your score is . . .

57-70
God apparently has given you a very strong appreciation for His unconditional love and acceptance. You seem to be free of the fear of failure that plagues most people. (Some people who score this high either are greatly deceived, or have become callous to their emotions as a way to suppress pain.)

47-56

The fear of failure controls your responses rarely or only in certain situations. Again, the only major exceptions are those who are not honest with themselves.

37-46

When you experience emotional problems, they may relate to a sense of failure or to some form of criticism. Upon reflection, you will probably relate many of your previous decisions to this fear. Many of your future decisions also will be affected by the fear of failure unless you take direct action to overcome it.

27-36

The fear of failure forms a general backdrop to your life. There are probably few days that you are not affected in some way by this fear. Unfortunately, this robs you of the joy and peace your salvation is meant to bring.

0-26

Experiences of failure dominate your memory and probably have resulted in a great deal of depression. These problems will remain until some definitive action is taken. In other words, this condition will not simply disappear; time alone cannot heal your pain. You need to experience deep healing in your self-concept, in your relationship with God and in your relationships with others.

Effects of the Fear of Failure

In the following exercise, we will examine the effects of the fear of failure, which stems from the false belief, *I must meet certain standards in order to feel good about myself.*

■ List two recent situations in which your performance did not measure up to the standard(s) you had set for yourself. Identify the standard(s) you felt you needed to meet. Then try to remember what thoughts and emotions accompanied each occasion, and the actions you took that reflected those thoughts and feelings:

Example
• Situation: *I failed to make a sale.*

- Standards: *I must meet my quota to feel good about myself.*

- Thoughts: *I'm a failure. I'll never make my quota. I'll never get promoted. I'll probably be fired any day now.*

- Emotions: fear, anger, depression

- Actions: *I avoided my boss for three days. I yelled at my wife and kids, taking out my anger on them.*

- SITUATION:

- Standards:

- Thoughts:

- Emotions:

- Actions:

- SITUATION:

- Standards:

- Thoughts:

- Emotions:

- Actions:

■ Do you see any patterns reflected in your emotions and actions? If so, what are they?

■ Why do people use performance as a measurement of personal worth?

■ Do you have to be successful in order to feel good about yourself? If so, what would you have to be or do to feel like you are a success?

• In what area(s) would you *never* allow yourself to fail?

■ Through what roles or activities (including Christian service) are you trying to gain a greater sense of self-worth?

■ Does performing these activities make you more pleasing to God?

■ How did your desire to meet certain standards affect your eating-disordered thinking and behavior?

■ How does that desire affect your relationships with others?

■ How do you feel toward those who hinder your ability to meet your standards?

■ What do you do to avoid failure?

■ How do you think your life would be different if you did not experience the fear of failure?

The fear of failure is like stacking marbles—a very difficult task, but not any more difficult than trying to win the performance game. When we evaluate ourselves by our performance, we're ultimately going to lose no matter how successful we are at the moment.

If we believe that our self-worth is based on our success, we will try to avoid failure at all costs. We will attempt only those things in which we are confident of success and avoid activities which pose a risk of failure. We will spend time around those who are not a threat to us and avoid people who, either by their greater success or by their disapproval of us, make us feel like failures.

Another consequence of needing to meet certain standards in order to feel good about ourselves is a rules-dominated life. Many of us know people who have a set of rules for everything, and who always place their attention on their performance. However, the focus of the gospel is on relationships, not regulations. Focusing only on rules will relegate our lives to the prison of self-examination.

On the other hand, we may be feeling very good about ourselves because we are winning the performance game. We may be so talented that we are reaching virtually every goal we have set for ourselves. We can't afford to mistake this pride for positive self-worth. We must realize that God is able to bring about whatever circumstances are necessary to cause us to stop trusting in ourselves. God intends to bring us to Himself through prayer and the study of His Word so that we can know, love and serve Him. Sometimes He will allow us to fail miserably so that we will look to Him instead of to ourselves for our security and significance. This is because God knows that any life less than He intended is a second-class existence. He loves you too much to let you continue to obtain your self-esteem from the empty promise of success.

God's Answer: Justification

As a result of Christ's death on the cross, our sins are forgiven and God has imputed Christ's righteousness to us. We have been *justified* by Christ and therefore, are fully pleasing to God.

■ Read Rom. 3:19-28; 4:4-5; 5:1-11. What does it mean to be *justified?*

164

■ Read 2 Cor. 5:21; Col. 1:22; 3:12 and Heb. 10:14. Are you as righteous, holy and blameless as Christ? Why or why not?

■ Read Rom. 3:9-23; 5:6-10 and Eph. 2:1-3. Why did you need to be justified and have Christ's righteousness attributed to you? Describe God's view of you before your justification:

■ How was your justification accomplished?
• Rom. 3:24; Titus 3:7

• Rom. 3:28; Gal. 2:16

• Rom. 5:1; Gal. 3:24

• Rom. 5:9; Heb. 9:22

■ What are the results of justification?
• Rom. 4:7-8

• Rom. 5:1, 9

• Rom. 8:1, 33-34

• 2 Cor. 5:14-15, 21

• Titus 3:7

■ Read Rom. 4:6-8 and Heb. 10:17. Are you remembering sins that God has forgotten? If so, why?

• Does remembering sin help you in any way? If so, how?

■ How does being justified and having Christ's righteousness lead you to the conclusion: *I am completely forgiven by God, and am fully pleasing to Him?*

■ If our good works won't make us more pleasing to God, why should we be involved in good works? (See Rom. 6:12-13; 1 Cor. 6:18-20; Col. 3:23-24 and Titus 2:11-14.)

■ Read Rom. 14:23; 1 Cor. 3:11-15; 10:31) What determines whether or not a deed will honor God?

■ Review the situations you described on page 162. Using one of the occasions you listed, chart how your behavior would have been different if you had believed the truth that you are completely forgiven by God, and are fully pleasing to Him, rather than the false belief, *I must meet certain standards in order to feel good about myself.*

• SITUATION:

• Belief: *I am both completely forgiven and fully pleasing to God.*

• Thoughts:

• Emotions:

• Actions:

■ Memorize Rom. 5:1.

If we base our self-worth on our ability to meet standards, we will try to compensate, either by avoiding risks or by trying to succeed no matter what the cost. Either way, failure looms as a constant enemy. But God has a solution for the fear of failure! He has given us a secure self-worth totally apart from our ability to perform. We have been forgiven through Christ's death on the cross, which paid for our sins. But God didn't stop with forgiving us; He also granted us the very righteousness of Christ!

Visualize two ledgers: on one is a list of all your sins; on the other, a list of the righteousness of Christ. Now exchange your ledger for Christ's. This exemplifies justification—transferring our sin to Christ and His righteousness to us. In 2 Cor. 5:21, Paul wrote: *He made Him* (Christ) *who knew no sin to be sin on our behalf, that we might become the righteousness of God in Him.*

Justification carries no guilt with it, and has no memory of past transgressions. Christ paid for all our sins at the cross—past, present and future. Hebrews 10:17 says, *And their sins and their lawless deeds I will remember know more.* We are completely forgiven by God! In the same act of love through which God forgave our sin, He also provided for our righteousness: the worthiness to stand in His presence. By imputing righteousness to us, God attributes Christ's worth to us. The moment we accept Christ, God no longer sees us as condemned sinners. Instead, we are forgiven, we receive Christ's righteousness and God sees us as creatures who are fully pleasing to Him.

God intended that Adam and his descendants be righteous people, fully experiencing His love and eternal purposes. But sin short-circuited that relationship. God's perfect payment for sin has since satisfied His righteous wrath, again enabling us to have that status of righteousness and to delight in knowing and honoring the Lord.

God desires for those of us who have been redeemed to experience the realities of His redemption. We are forgiven and righteous because of Christ's sacrifice; therefore, we are pleasing to God in spite of our failures. This reality can replace our fear of failure with peace, hope and joy. Failure need not be a millstone around our necks. Neither success nor failure is the proper basis of our self-worth. Christ alone is the source of our forgiveness, freedom, joy and purpose.

Approval Addict

Living by the false belief, *I must be approved by certain others to feel good about myself,* causes us to fear rejection continually, and to conform virtually all of our attitudes and actions to the expectations of others. How are you affected by this belief? Take the following test to determine how strongly you fear rejection.

Fear of Rejection Test

Read the following statements. Look at the top of the test and choose the term which best describes your response. Put the number above that term in the blank beside each statement.

1	2	3	4	5	6	7
Always	Very Often	Often	Sometimes	Seldom	Very Seldom	Never

_____ 1. I avoid certain people.

_____ 2. When I sense that someone might reject me, I become nervous and anxious.

_____ 3. I am uncomfortable around those who are different from me.

_____ 4. It bothers me when someone is unfriendly to me.

_____ 5. I am basically shy and unsocial.

_____ 6. I am critical of others.

_____ 7. I find myself trying to impress others.

_____ 8. I become depressed when someone criticizes me.

_____ 9. I always try to determine what people think of me.

_____ 10. I don't understand people and what motivates them.

_____ Total (Add up the numbers you have placed in the blanks.)

Interpretation of Score
If your score is . . .

57-70

God apparently has given you a strong appreciation for His unconditional love and acceptance. You seem to be free of the fear of rejection that plagues most people. (Some people who score this high either are greatly deceived, or have become callous to their emotions as a way to suppress pain.)

47-56

The fear of rejection controls your responses rarely or only in certain situations. Again, the only major exceptions are those who are not honest with themselves.

37-46

When you experience emotional problems, they may relate to a sense of rejection. Upon reflection, you probably will relate many of your previous decisions to this fear. Many of your future decisions also will be affected by the fear of rejection unless you take direct action to overcome it.

27-36

The fear of rejection forms a general backdrop to your life. There are probably few days that you are not in some way affected by this fear. Unfortunately, this robs you of the joy and peace your salvation is meant to bring.

0-26

Experiences of rejection dominate your memory and probably have resulted in a great deal of depression. These problems will persist until some definitive action is taken. In other words, this condition will not simply disappear; time alone cannot heal your pain. You need to experience deep healing in your self-concept, in your relationship with God and in your relationships with others.

Effects of the Fear of Rejection

The following exercise is designed to help you understand the fear of rejection and the resulting false belief, *I must be approved by certain others to feel good about myself.*

■ Are you adversely affected by anyone's disrespect or disapproval? If so, list those individuals or groups:

■ To see how others' expectations can affect you, select one of the people in the above question and answer the following:

• _____ would be more pleased with me if I would:

   a)

   b)

   c)

• _____ is proud of me when I:

   a)

   b)

   c)

• How does _____ attempt to get me to change by what he or she says and does?

   a)

   b)

   c)

• Things I do or say to get _____ to approve of me include:

   a)

   b)

   c)

(Use a separate sheet of paper for each of the people or groups you listed on page 169.)

■ List several specific instances when others (friends, boss, parents) have withheld approval, or have used criticism, silence or sarcasm to get you to do what they wanted you to do. What did they say or do? Did they succeed? Why or why not?

-

-

-

-

■ Can you recall specific instances in which the fear of rejection influenced your moral standards (drinking, drug abuse, theft, lying, sexual behavior, lifestyle, etc.)? List those instances and explain how the fear of rejection affected your behavior.

■ If you run from rejection, who really is in control of your life?

■ How have you used disapproval, silence, sarcasm or criticism to get others to do what you wanted them to do?

■ How did you use different aspects of your eating disorder to get others to do what you wanted them to do? Be specific.

■ Sometimes, rather than praising others because we genuinely appreciate them, we use praise as a form of manipulation. Our motive is to influence them to do something we want them to do.

- How do you feel when people praise you only to manipulate you?

- Have you used praise to manipulate others? If so, why, and how have you used it?

- How could manipulating others by praising them be considered a form of rejection?

For whatever reason and to whatever degree we have experienced rejection, our fear of going through that pain again can affect us profoundly. We learn how to deal with physical injury early in life, but because emotional pain is sometimes perceived as a sign of weakness, and because we have not learned how to respond appropriately to this pain, we avoid it. If we are hurt, we may attempt to deny our pain by ignoring it. We may drive ourselves to accomplish tasks, hoping to earn the approval and recognition of others. Some of us can't say no for this reason. Or, we may become passive, withdrawing from others and avoiding those decisions and activities which others might criticize, or which can't guarantee success for us. Usually, our goal in these instances is to avoid the pain of rejection by not doing anything which might be objectionable, but this also prevents us from enjoying the pleasures of healthy relationships and achievements.

Other behaviors related to the fear of rejection include:

1. being easily manipulated.
2. being hypersensitive to criticism.
3. acting defensively.
4. showing hostility toward those who disagree with us.
5. pursuing superficial relationships.
6. exaggerating or minimizing the truth to impress people.
7. exhibiting shyness.
8. being passive.
9. having a nervous breakdown.

Evaluating our self-worth by what we and others think of our performance leads us to believe that any time our performance is unacceptable, we also are unacceptable. To some extent, virtually all of us have internalized the following sentence into our belief system, and hold to it with amazing tenacity: *I must have acceptance, respect and approval in order to have self-worth.* This is the basic false belief behind all peer pressure.

Rejection can be communicated in a number of ways. Not only do criticism, sarcasm and silence convey this message, but praise—when used as a form of manipulation—also is a form of rejection. We must ask ourselves what we are trying to accomplish when we praise someone. What is our goal? If we desire to help the person, to build him or her up and to instill encouragement through appreciation, then praise is a godly form of communication. But if our desire is to get someone else to assist in accomplishing our goals, to contribute to our program or to help us look good in front of others, then praise is a subtle but powerful form of rejection. Unfortunately, many of us fall prey to this manipulative praise because we so desperately want to be appreciated, and often will do whatever it takes to get it from others.

If you realize that you manipulate others through praise, confess it as sin and choose to seek their good instead of your goal. Be willing to ask, *What am I trying to accomplish?* in your interaction with others, and strive to communicate genuine, heartfelt appreciation because Christ has given them worth by sacrificing His life for them.

There are four basic levels of acceptance and rejection. Understanding these will help you understand the nature of your relationships with other people, concerning both how you are treated and how you treat them. Each centers around the question: What does one have to do to be accepted?

1. *Total Rejection*: "No matter what you do, it's not good enough." Example: relationships characterized by deep bitterness or hurt.
2. *Highly-Conditional Acceptance*: "You must meet certain requirements to be accepted." Examples: most jobs, relationships with demanding people.
3. *Mildly-Conditional Acceptance*: "I will be happier with you if you do these things." Examples: most marriages, parent-child relationships and friendships.
4. *Unconditional Acceptance*: "I love you and accept you no matter what you do. There is nothing you can do that can make me stop loving you." (This does not mean that we can do as we please or that we are to ignore unacceptable behavior in others. Unconditional acceptance may include loving confrontation, correction, and in some cases, discipline. The focus here is on the individual rather than on his or her behavior.) Examples: God, and typically, relationships in which one person's needs are not dependent on the other's.

■ Make a list of the major relationships in your life: family members, friends, people in your school, office, church, etc. How does each of these people tend to treat you? How do you tend to treat each of them?

How should you respond to each of them? How can you put fewer demands and conditions on your acceptance of them?

God's Answer: Reconciliation

God's answer to the pain of rejection is reconciliation. Christ died for our sins and restored us to a proper relationship with God. He accepts us completely as His own!

■ Define *reconcile*. (Use a dictionary if necessary.)

• Who caused the alienation in your relationship with God (Is. 53:6; 59:2; Rom. 3:9-12)?

■ Read Eph. 2:1-3 and 2 Thess. 1:8-9. How severe was the barrier between you and Holy God?

■ Read Col. 1:21-22. Compare your former state to your present condition in Christ:

■ Read Rom. 5:8-11. Who initiated the restoration of your relationship with God?

• How did God reconcile you to Himself?

• What is your response to God? (What does "to exult" mean?)

■ What is wrong with the statement, *Thank You, Lord, for accepting me even though I am so unacceptable*?

• Are you currently acceptable?
• To what degree are you acceptable?
• To whom are you acceptable?
• Why are you acceptable?

■ If you are completely and fully accepted by the perfect Creator of the universe, why is it still so painful to be rejected by other people?

174

■ Read John 17:19-26 and 20:17 to see the extent of your reconciliation to God.
• Whom does the Father love more: Jesus Christ or you?
• How does Christ refer to you in John 20:17?
• How do these verses make you feel?

■ Can you think of two recent situations in which you felt rejected, or in which someone disapproved of something you said or did? If so, list them. Describe your response. How would your response have been different if you had believed the truth of your total acceptance in Christ?

• SITUATION:

• Your Response:

• How Believing the Truth Would Have Changed Your Response:

• SITUATION:

• Your Response:

• How Believing the Truth Would Have Changed Your Response:

■ Memorize Col. 1:21-22.

When God chose to redeem us so that we could relate to Him and rule with Him, He did not make us partially righteous, nor has He allowed for our righteousness to be marred by poor performance. The blood of Christ is sufficient to pay for all sin. Because of His blood, we are holy and righteous before God, even in the midst of sin. This does not minimize the inherent destructiveness of sin, but glorifies the indescribable sacrifice of Christ.

There is no biblical tenet more neglected in its practical application than the doctrine of reconciliation. The Colossians' reference to this doctrine reveals its application to us:

> *And although you were formerly alienated and hostile*
> *in your mind, engaged in evil deeds,*

175

> *yet He has now reconciled you in His fleshly body*
> *through death, in order to present you before Him holy and*
> *blameless and beyond reproach . . . .*
>
> Col. 1:21-22

Relish those last words. God sees us as holy and blameless and beyond reproach at this very moment. This is not merely a reference to our future standing; it describes our present status as well. We are totally accepted by God.

God received us into a loving, intimate, personal relationship with Him at the moment we placed our faith in Christ. We are united with God in an eternal and inseparable bond (Rom. 8:38-39). We are born of God in an indissoluble union as fellow heirs with Christ. Recognizing that no sin can make a Christian unacceptable to God is God-honoring faith in a blood-sealed warrant with the Holy Spirit, *who is given as a pledge of our inheritance, with a view to the redemption of God's own possession . . .* (Eph. 1:14).

Because our relationship with God was bought entirely by the blood of Christ, no amount of good works can make us more acceptable to Him. Titus 3:5 says: *He saved us, not on the basis of deeds which we have done in righteousness, but according to His mercy . . . .* Because Christ has reconciled us to God, we can experience the incredible truth that we are totally accepted by God.

What should we do when we have failed or when someone disapproves of us? A practical way of summarizing the truth we've examined is: *It would be nice if _____ (my boss liked me, I could fix the refrigerator, my complexion were clear, James had picked me up on time, or . . .), but I'm still deeply loved, completely forgiven, fully pleasing, totally accepted and complete in Christ.*

This statement doesn't mean that we won't feel pain or anger when we're rejected. We need to be honest about our feelings. A statement like the one above is simply a quick way to gain God's perspective on our situation. It is not magic, but it enables us to reflect on the implications of biblical truth. We can apply this truth in every difficult situation, whether it involves someone else's disapproval or failure, or our own failure to accomplish something. Memorize the truth in the above statement and begin to apply it in your situations and relationships.

The Blame Game

The false belief, *Those who fail (including me) are unworthy of love and deserve to be punished,* is at the root of our fear of punishment and propensity to punish others. Take the test below to determine how much you are influenced by this lie.

Fear of Punishment/Punishing Others Test

Read the following statements. Look at the top of the test and choose the term which best describes your response. Put the number above that term in the blank beside each statement.

1	2	3	4	5	6	7
Always	Very Often	Often	Sometimes	Seldom	Very Seldom	Never

_____ 1. I fear what God might do to me.

_____ 2. After I fail, I worry about God's response.

_____ 3. When I see someone in a difficult situation, I wonder what he or she did to deserve it.

_____ 4. When something goes wrong, I have a tendency to think that God must be punishing me.

_____ 5. I am very hard on myself when I fail.

_____ 6. I find myself wanting to blame others when they fail.

_____ 7. I get angry with God when someone who is immoral or dishonest prospers.

_____ 8. I am compelled to tell others when I see them doing wrong.

_____ 9. I tend to focus on the faults and failures of others.

_____10. God seems harsh to me.

_____ Total (Add up the numbers you have placed in the blanks.)

Interpretation of Score

If your score is . . .

57-70

God apparently has given you a very strong appreciation for His unconditional love and acceptance. You seem to be free of the fear of punishment that plagues most people. (Some people who score this high either are greatly deceived, or have become callous to their emotions as a way to suppress pain.)

47-56

The fear of punishment and the compulsion to punish others control your responses rarely or only in certain situations. Again, the only exceptions are those who are not honest with themselves.

37-46

When you experience emotional problems, they may relate to a fear of punishment or to an inner urge to punish others. Upon reflection, you probably will relate many of your previous decisions to this fear. Many of your future decisions also will be affected by the fear of punishment and/ or the compulsion to punish others unless you take direct action to overcome these tendencies.

27-36

The fear of punishment forms a general backdrop to your life. There are probably few days that you are not affected in some way by the fear of punishment and the propensity to blame others. Unfortunately, this robs you of the joy and peace your salvation is meant to bring.

0-26

Experiences of punishment dominate your memory, and you probably have experienced a great deal of depression. These problems will remain until some definitive plan is followed. In other words, this condition will not simply disappear; time alone cannot heal your pain. You need to experience deep healing in your self-concept, in your relationship with God and in your relationships with others.

Effects of the Fear of Punishment and Propensity to Punish Others

This exercise will help you understand the fear of punishment and the false belief, *Those who fail are unworthy of love and deserve to be blamed and condemned.*

■ Do you really deserve to feel good about yourself? Why or why not?

■ Describe three recent incidents in your life in which you feared being blamed or punished. What prompted this fear?

1.

2.

3.

■ Do you spend much time thinking about your weaknesses and failures? If so, why? (List as many reasons as you can.)

• What are the three most negative terms you use to describe yourself?

■ Does condemning yourself help you to be a better person? Why or why not?

■ Think of a close friend or family member with whom you've had a conflict. What did you say or do to inflict emotional pain?

• What are some reasons you said or did those things?

■ After sinning, do you ever believe you have to feel badly about yourself before you can feel good about yourself? If so, list some of the situations in which you've done this:

■ Do you want to go to the Father after you've sinned? Why or why not?

■ If something goes wrong, do you assume the Lord is punishing you?

■ Does God punish His children?

The proof of blame's effectiveness is that we use it so often. We often believe that we deserve to be blamed for any significant shortcoming, and think self-inflicted punishment will clear us of guilt and enable us to feel good about ourselves again. Why?

We have been conditioned to accept personal blame or condemnation every time our performance is unsatisfactory. For example, do you generally have an urge to find out who is at fault when something fails? Do you look for excuses when you fail?

Rather than evaluating our problems objectively, most of us tend to defend ourselves. Counterattack triggers counterattack. The more we criticize other people, the more defensive they usually get, and the less likely they are to admit their errors (especially to us). Criticism can lead to a counterattack from both sides, and pretty soon it's like a volleyball game, with each person intensifying the pace while returning blame to the other person's side.

However, it is sometimes even more destructive for people to accept blame without defending themselves. Tom was becoming an emotional zombie under his wife's incessant condemnation, but instead of fighting back, he kept thinking, *Yes, Suzanne's right. I am an incompetent fool.* He was like the worn-out punching bag of a heavyweight fighter.

Both self-inflicted punishment and the compulsion to punish others result from the false belief: *Those who fail are unworthy of love and deserve to be blamed and condemned.*

God's Answer: Propitiation

At the cross, God poured out His wrath against sin. This exercise will help you see that God's wrath has been satisfied; therefore, we have no need to fear punishment.

■ Define *propitiation*. (Use a dictionary if necessary.)

■ We each have committed an incalculable number of sinful (disobedient, self-centered) thoughts and actions. How many sins can a Holy God overlook?

■ Read Ezek. 7:8-9; Rom. 2:4-5 and Eph. 2:1-3. Does God's wrath have a specific object? If so, what is it?

■ Read Gen. 19:1-26; Jer. 4:4; Ezek. 5:11-17; 23:22-30 and 2 Thess. 1:6-10. List some characteristics of God's wrath from these passages:

■ Read 1 John 4:9-10.
• Are you loved by the Father?
• How do you know you are loved?
• Do you feel loved?

■ Consider what it would be like to experience the wrath of Almighty God, and then read Is. 53:4-10. Place your name in the place of appropriate pronouns ("Surely he took up_____'s infirmities" [NIV]). The wrath that you deserved has been poured out on Christ.

• In what ways can you express gratitude to Christ for what He has done for you?

■ The more we understand God's love and forgiveness, the more we will be willing and able to forgive others. If we think about it, the things that others do to us are all trivial in comparison to our sin of rebellion against God that He has graciously forgiven. This is why Paul encouraged the Ephesian Christians to forgive each other *just as God in Christ also has forgiven you* (Eph. 4:32), completely and willingly.

• Are there any sins (or even personality differences) in others that you have difficulty forgiving? If so, list them and confess to God your lack of forgiveness:

• How do these compare to your sins that deserved God's wrath, but received the payment of Christ's substitutionary death?

■ Memorize 1 John 4:9-10.

God's plan for us is centered in the cross. To understand His plan, we must first understand the meaning of propitiation.

Prior to our spiritual birth, even our good deeds were despicable to God (Is. 64:6). If we are honest about our performance, we must admit that we have sinned thousands of times, even after having accepted Christ. The problem with our sinfulness is that God is absolutely holy, pure and perfect. *God is light, and in Him there is no darkness at all* (1 John 1:5). Because God is holy, He cannot overlook or compromise with sin. It took one sin to separate Adam from God. For God to condone even one sin would instantly defile His holiness, which He indicates by His righteous condemnation of sin (Rom. 6:23).

The Father did not escape witnessing His Son's mistreatment: the mocking, the scourging and the cross. He could have spoken and ended the whole ordeal, yet He kept silent, choosing to allow it to continue so that we could be saved. What an expression of love! Its depth is incomprehensible.

Many of us cannot fully appreciate God's love and forgiveness because these words often are misused and misunderstood in our language and culture today. In addition, many of us have a distorted concept of the heavenly Father. We believe that He is thrilled when we accept Christ and are born into His family, but that He is proud of us only for as long as we perform well, and that the better our performance, the more He loves us.

In reality, God loves us, and not a moment goes by that He isn't thinking loving thoughts about us (Ps. 40:5). We are His children, and are individually special to Him because of Christ!

Love and *forgiveness* will redefine themselves for us as we experience God's loving work in our lives, and as we recognize and personalize the Lord's willingness to suffer pain and experience death on the cross—*for me*. By developing a "heart knowledge" of the fact that there is no hiding from God, that He sees all of our sin in all of its ugliness, and that He was willing to bear the penalty for that sin in His own physical body so that we would not have to, we will better understand what the phrase "unconditional love" means. In His mercy, He deliberately chooses our salvation over our just punishment. Rather than punish and condemn us, He chooses to accept, love and forgive us.

We can be like Him! As we discovered in step 5, Jesus said that to forgive and love others is to be perfect, like Him (Matt. 5:43-48). When we receive His forgiveness and learn to forgive others, then we reflect a portion of God's nature and glory.

God loves you and enjoys revealing His love to you. He enjoys being loved by you, but He knows that you can love Him only if you are experiencing His love for you. Propitiation means that Jesus Christ has satisfied the Father's righteous condemnation of sin by His death. The Scriptures give only one reason to explain this incredible fact: God loves you!

Shame

When we base our self-worth on past failures, dissatisfaction with personal appearance or bad habits, we often develop a fourth false belief: *I am what I am. I cannot change. I am hopeless.* This lie binds people to the hopeless pessimism associated with poor self-esteem. Take the following test to establish how strongly you experience shame.

Shame Test
Read the statements below. Look at the top of the test and choose the term which best describes your response. Put the number above that term in the blank beside each statement.

1	2	3	4	5	6	7
Always	Very Often	Often	Sometimes	Seldom	Very Seldom	Never

_____ 1. I often think about past failures or experiences of rejection.

_____ 2. There are certain things about my past which I cannot recall without experiencing strong, painful emotions (guilt, shame, anger, fear, etc.).

_____ 3. I seem to make the same mistakes over and over again.

_____ 4. There are certain aspects of my character I want to change, but I don't believe I can ever successfully do so.

_____ 5. I feel inferior.

_____ 6. There are aspects of my appearance that I cannot accept.

_____ 7. I am generally disgusted with myself.

_____ 8. I feel that certain experiences have basically ruined my life.

_____ 9. I perceive myself as an immoral person.

_____10. I feel I have lost the opportunity to experience a complete and wonderful life.

_____ Total (Add up the numbers you have placed in the blanks.)

Interpretation of Score
If your score is . . .

57-70
God apparently has given you a strong appreciation for His unconditional love and acceptance. You seem to be free of the shame that plagues most people. (Some people who score this high either are greatly deceived, or have become callous to their emotions as a way to suppress pain.)

47-56

Shame controls your responses rarely or only in certain situations. Again, the exceptions are those who are not honest with themselves.

36-46

When you experience emotional problems, they may relate to a sense of shame. Upon reflection, you probably will relate many of your previous decisions to a poor sense of self-worth. Many of your future decisions also will be affected by low self-esteem unless you take direct action to overcome it.

27-36

Shame forms a generally negative backdrop to your life. There probably are few days in which you are not affected in some way by shame. Unfortunately, this robs you of the joy and peace your salvation was meant to bring.

0-26

Experiences of shame dominate your memory and probably have resulted in a great deal of depression. These problems will remain until some definitive action is taken. In other words, this condition will not simply disappear one day; time alone cannot heal your pain. You must deal with its root issue.

Effects of Shame

This exercise examines the shame that can arise from a negative evaluation of our past performance and/or our physical appearance. Shame leads to the false belief: *I am what I am. I cannot change. I am hopeless.*

■ Define *shame*:

■ When do you experience shame?

■ In what ways does shame make an impact on our sense of self-worth? How does shame lock us into a low opinion of ourselves?

■ Is there anything you can't keep from doing? When you've tried to stop but then do it again, how do you feel about yourself?

■ List aspects of your appearance or past performance which prevent you from viewing yourself as a fully pleasing and totally accepted person.

• Appearance:

• Past Performance:

■ When people with a poor self-concept succeed at something, one would think that they would be encouraged and have a more positive outlook. Often, however, pessimistic people explain or minimize their success and continue in their hopelessness.

• Do you do this when you succeed?

• If so, what do you say to others and yourself?

• Why do you say those things?

■ What sources of input reinforce this low view of yourself?

■ Read Ps. 139:13-16. What was God's involvement in the formation of your physical appearance and personality?

■ If you have a poor self-concept, what do you think it will take to overcome it and experience the joy and power of your new life in Christ?

■ How do you think other people would describe you?

• What are their expectations of you?

• How have their expectations affected your self-esteem?

Shame often results from instances of neglect or abuse, and then is reinforced by failures in our performance or "flaws" in our appearance. Even when others don't know of our failure, we assume their opinion of us is poor and adopt what we think that opinion might be.

If we base our self-worth on our performance long enough, our past behavior will eventually become the sole basis of our worth. We will see ourselves with certain character qualities and flaws because that's the way we always have been. We then will have unconsciously incorporated Satan's lie into our belief system: *I must always be what I have been and live with whatever self-worth I have, because that's just me.* Interestingly, we claim that only our poor behavior is "just me." We never hear anyone say, "That's just me. I'm so wonderful, honest and bright."

We may think that self-depreciation is humility, but true humility is an accurate appraisal of our worth in Christ: We deserved God's righteous condemnation, yet we are recipients of His unconditional love, grace and righteousness through Christ. We are deeply loved, completely forgiven, fully pleasing, totally accepted and complete in Him. Thankfulness, generosity, kindness and confidence constitute true humility!

Another aspect of a poor self-concept relates to personal appearance. Most of us would like to change some aspect of our appearance, but we really can't alter much about the way we look. We may not only base our self-worth on our appearance, but may tend to base our acceptance of others on their appearance, even the color of their skin. We may never be any more cruel than when we accept or reject others based on their appearance.

Are you angry with God for the way He made you? Do you compare and rank your appearance with that of others? If you do, you will suffer at some point because someone always will be prettier, stronger, cuter or more handsome than you are. Even if you are spectacularly beautiful or strikingly handsome, you will suffer because you will be afraid of losing your good looks, the basis of your self-worth.

If we insist on valuing our worth by our appearance and performance, sooner or later God will graciously allow us to see the futility of that struggle. God created our needs for a sense of significance. He therefore knows that we never will come to Him until we find that people's opinions are empty and meaningless. At that point, we can turn to Him and find comfort and encouragement in the truths of His Word.

God's Answer: Regeneration

This exercise will help you see yourself as a new creature in Christ, with new potential and new capacities. The truth that you have been made new in Christ will enable you to develop a strong, positive self-esteem in spite of "flaws" in your appearance or failures in your past.

■ Do you really think that you can view yourself any differently than you always have? If not, why?

■ Read 2 Cor. 5:17.
   • Define *regeneration*. (Use a dictionary if necessary.)

   • What does your having been made a new creature mean to you?

■ How was your regeneration accomplished?

   • John 1:12-13

   • John 3:16

   • Titus 3:5

   • 1 Pet. 1:3

   • 1 Pet. 1:23

■ Read Eph. 4:22-24 and Col. 3:9-10. What process do you need to complete in order to experience your new self?

■ On the following page, list characteristics of your old and new self based on the passages given there.

CHARACTERISTICS OF MY NEW SELF	CHARACTERISTICS OF MY OLD SELF
Rom 6:18	Rom. 8:16-17
1 Cor. 12:27; Eph. 5:30	2 Cor. 5:21
2 Cor. 5:17	Gal. 5:22-23
Gal. 5:19-21	Eph. 4:23-32
Eph. 4:17-22	Col. 2:10
Col. 3:5-9	Col. 3:10-15
Titus 3:3	1 Pet. 1:16

■ Read Rom. 6:12-23 and 1 Cor. 6:9-11. How does the truth of regeneration free you from evaluating yourself by your past performance?

■ Read 1 Sam. 16:6-7 and Ps. 139:13-16. How does the truth of regeneration free you from the shame of flaws in your physical appearance?

■ How could understanding your newness in Christ affect your personal fitness or grooming habits?

■ How can knowing that you have a new life in Christ affect the way you think, feel and act?

■ Do you use past failures, your appearance or some other "flaw" as an excuse for not living for Christ? If so, what is your excuse? How valid is it?

■ Memorize 2 Cor. 5:17.

Regeneration is the renewing work of the Holy Spirit by which a person literally becomes a new creation. Our regeneration occurred at the instant of our conversion to Christ. At that moment, we were given more than a change of direction; our inner spirit received the impartation of new life. Jesus called this a new birth in John 3:3, 5-6: *That which is born of the flesh is flesh, and that which is born of the Spirit is spirit* (John 3:6). Regeneration is the Spirit-wrought renewal of our human spirit, a transforming resuscitation so that *the spirit is alive* within us (Rom. 8:10).

The Holy Spirit has been joined to our human spirit, forming a new spiritual entity. A new birth has produced a new being. *Therefore, if any man is in Christ, he is a new creature; the old things passed away; behold, new things have come* (2 Cor. 5:17). Study these words carefully. Ephesians 4:24 says that our new self *has* (already) *been created in righteousness and holiness of the truth.* However, we must yet "put on" this new self in order to produce godly thoughts and actions—as the acorn produces an oak tree!

What is the basis of your self-worth? Are you living by scriptural truths or by false beliefs? False beliefs are all a part of Satan's insidious plan. By now, you may see deception as a part of his scheme to steal, and kill and destroy mankind. In order to prevent him from victimizing us with lies, it will be helpful not only to recognize and reject them, but to replace them with the truth of God's Word.

The following exercises provide some steps we can take to reject Satan's lies and replace them with a stronghold of truth in our minds.

■ Making a Truth Card

- A simple 3x5 card can be a key factor in helping you base your self-worth on the liberating truths of the Scriptures. On the front, write out both the following truths and their corresponding verses from Scripture. On the back of the card, write out the four false beliefs.

I am deeply loved by God (1 John 4:9-10).
I am completely forgiven, and am fully pleasing to God (Rom. 5:1).
I am totally accepted by God (Col. 1:21-22).
I am a new creation—complete in Christ (2 Cor. 5:17).

Carry this card with you continuously. Each time you are about to do a routine activity, like having something to drink, look at the front side and slowly meditate on each phrase. Thank the Lord for making you into a person who has these qualities. By doing this for the next twenty-eight days, you will develop a habit of remembering that you are deeply loved, completely forgiven, fully pleasing, totally accepted and complete in Christ.

If you haven't already done so, memorize the supporting verses listed on the card over the next four days. Look in your Bible for other verses that support these truths and commit them to memory. Doing this will establish God's Word as the basis for these truths (Col. 3:16). Also memorize the false beliefs. The more familiar you are with these lies, the more you will be able to recognize them in your thoughts. Then, as you recognize them, you can more readily replace them with the truths of God's Word.

■ Exposing Ungodly Thoughts

Our thoughts reveal what we really believe, yet it is difficult for most of us to be objective in our thinking simply because we haven't trained ourselves to be. We usually let any and every thought run its course in our minds without analyzing its worth. Is it a God-honoring thought, or is it a *speculation*, or a *lofty thing raised up against the knowledge of God*? (2 Cor. 10:5).

As we grow in our knowledge of God's Word, we will increase our ability to identify thoughts that reflect Satan's deceptions. Then, we can reject those lies and replace them with scriptural truth, just as our Lord did when He was tempted by Satan in the wilderness (Matt. 4:1-11). One way of identifying deceptive thoughts is to state what is true and see what comes to mind. Hopefully, our thoughts will increasingly reflect our thankfulness to God for who He is and what He has done for us, but sometimes we will respond by contradicting the truth.

For example, you might respond to the truth that you are fully pleasing to God by thinking, *No, I'm not! I mess up all the time, and to be fully pleasing, I'd have to be perfect!* When we see it written out, we more easily recognize that response as a lie.

As a first step in this analysis, write down your thoughts in response to the four truths we've examined. (Again, they probably will be mixed: some positive, thankful and godly, and some contradictory to the truth.)

• *I am deeply loved by God:*

• *I am both completely forgiven and fully pleasing to God:*

• *I am totally accepted by God:*

• *I am complete in Christ:*

Thoughts that contradict these truths are lies. Reject them and replace them with passages of Scripture to reinforce the truth in your mind. Here are some passages to reflect on:

Propitiation: Matt. 18:21-35; Luke 7:36-50; Rom. 3:25; 8:1-8; Col. 3:12-14; Heb. 2:17.
Justification: Rom. 3:19-24; 4:4-5; 5:1-11; Titus 2:11-14; 3:4-7.
Reconciliation: John 15:14-16; Rom. 5:8-10; Eph. 2:11-18.
Regeneration: 2 Cor. 5:17; Gal. 5:16-24; Eph. 2:4-5; 4:22-24; Col. 3:5-17.

As we gain a greater awareness of the battle within us between the Spirit and the flesh, and as we identify false beliefs that prompt sinful behavior and then renew our minds with the truth of God's Word, we can confidently ask God to remove our sinful patterns of behavior and begin to live in His resurrection power. It is true that we will never be sinless until we reign with Him in His kingdom, but as we grow in Him, we will sin less.

For Additional Reflection and Application

The truth card you made earlier is a "carry-around" statement of who we are in Christ—who He has planned and created us to be. Several years ago, Rapha's James Mahoney, Th.D., wrote the following as an expression of the truth about us as God has revealed it. You may wish to copy this and carry it with you. Its truth about you is profound and one that you need to remember and share with others, for whom it also is true.

Declaration
Because of Christ's redemption,
I am a new creation
of infinite worth.

I am deeply loved,
I am completely forgiven,
I am fully pleasing,
I am totally accepted by God.
I am absolutely complete in Christ.

When my performance
reflects my new identity in Christ,
that reflection is dynamically unique.

There has never been another person like me
in the history of mankind,
nor will there ever be.
God has made me an original,
one of a kind, a special person.

Self-esteem means to really know and believe what God has made and declared us to be—not just these bodies of clay, or the transient nature of our performance. In Christ, we are worth so much more than the *best* of our performance—how much more, then, are we worth than our negative performance? Step 7 shows us that we can do well without pride—we can have godly self-esteem and humility!

Step Eight
My Honest "Amends-ments"

We make a list of all persons we have harmed, and become willing to make amends to them all.

And just as you want men to treat you,
treat them in the same way.

Luke 6:31

Eating-disordered behavior, we have observed, has been a part of our strategy to deny strong emotions like fear and anger, and prevent them from gaining access into our lives and behavior. The fact that we often refrain from lashing out in our rage does not, contrary to our thinking, make us morally superior to those with whom we are angry. We are quite capable of nursing years-old grudges, hatreds, jealousies and secret rages. This accumulated wrath is a powerful vehicle to carry our eating disorder. Recovery therefore requires that we settle the business of internalizing and denying our unwelcome emotions, once and for all.

Forgiveness means deliberately choosing to give up our right to blame, condemn, find fault, punish and retaliate against others. It does not mean forgetting an offense or excusing it away; it means dealing with the offense as it is—raw, ugly and painful though that might be. It means giving up the right to binge/purge the rage away; it means giving up the right to some passive-aggressive form of retaliation, like procrastination, avoidance or the "silent treatment." It means putting aside our pride (there's that word again!), dealing with the offense in humility (and there's that word again!), thereby ceasing to carry the burden of the memory of the offender and the offense, so that we may get on with our lives. Make no mistake: As long as we harbor a grudge against another person for his or her offense, no matter how long ago it happened, we carry the full weight of the offense, and thus it seems that we carry the weight of the offender as well. How many hurting people go to their graves, forever encumbered by the weight of chains presented by dated offenses and former offenders, because they have failed to exercise forgiveness!

Often, our addiction acts as a metaphor for this very problem: Perhaps we eat compulsively and gain weight, symbolically adding new "blamings" to ourselves. Perhaps we obsess about body weight, insisting that we are "fat" when we are near death from starvation and really are weighted down by our wrath against the perpetrators of past wrongs in our lives. Or perhaps we desperately try to purge the wrath and shame that have accumulated from being victimized by truly vicious people in our past. What ponderous burdens we carry!

Just as importantly, our unwillingness to forgive others blocks our ability to experience God's forgiveness, thereby maintaining and perpetuating deep feelings of shame and self-loathing, fueling our old cycles of performance, perfectionism and despair. It is time we sought liberation from this bondage! Thus, we arrive at step 8.

Many of us experience great anxiety when faced with the eighth step because our minds are already racing to step 9, where we will actually begin to make amends. However, the purpose of step 8 is simply to *identify* those we harmed as a result of our addiction, and improve our understanding of the responsibility we have in our relationships with them.

One of these responsibilities is forgiveness. We know that we have been forgiven by God, and step 5 taught us the value of being accepted by another human being. In step 8, we will examine the practice of forgiving other people by preparing to ask them to forgive us.

Some of us will want to dodge this responsibility on the basis that our inappropriate response to someone else was just giving him or her what was deserved, or because we think *we* deserved something we wouldn't have gotten otherwise.

Paul wrote these words to the Roman Christians of the early Church:

> *Never pay back evil for evil to anyone. Respect what is right in the sight of all men.*
> *If possible, so far as it depends on you, be at peace with all men.*
> *Never take your own revenge, beloved, but leave room for the wrath of God, for it is written, "Vengeance is Mine, I will repay," says the Lord.*
>
> Rom. 12:17-19

■ What does it mean to you to be *at peace with all men*?

■ How would your life be different if you allowed God to take care of your grievances, rather than trying to take revenge on someone else yourself?

Forgiveness

As we mentioned earlier, one of the benefits we experienced in step 5 was acceptance. Once we have gained someone else's acceptance, it is easier to accept and forgive other people. In fact, our ability to extend grace and forgiveness is directly proportional to the degree we have personally experienced it ourselves.

When we have an eating disorder, our addiction serves to effectively blind us from negative emotions and repress feelings of resentment until the Holy Spirit reveals them to us.

Are there people you don't like to be around? . . . or whom you can't look in the eye? . . . or with whom you get angry every time you even think of them?

The following exercise is designed to help you extend the forgiveness God has given you to other people.

■ Read Matt. 18:21-35.
  • How great was the debt of the king's servant?
  • Was it possible for him ever to repay it?

■ Likewise, before you trusted Christ, how great was your debt to God for your sin? Was it possible for you ever to repay it?

■ What did the servant ask for?

  • What did the king grant him?

■ Why was the king's servant so harsh with his fellow servant over such a small debt?

■ Read Luke 7:36-50 (especially verse 47) and compare it with the parable in Matt. 18:21-35. What is the foundation for being able to love and forgive others?

197

■ Read Eph. 4:32 and Col. 3:12-13.
  • To what degree are we to forgive others?

  • Describe how God has forgiven you:

■ What are some of the effects people experience when they fail to forgive (attitudes toward others, opinion of themselves, quality of relationships, etc.)?

■ Do your answers to the above questions correspond to any effects of failing to forgive in your life? In your attitude toward others? Toward yourself? If so, explain:

■ Is there any particular sin for which you haven't experienced God's forgiveness? If so, what do you need in order to do so?

Being offended by others is a frequent experience in life. We go through periods when it seems that almost everybody is letting us down. We want freedom from being offended but the beat goes on. We are hurt by both our experience of the offense and our reliving of it. In fact, the initial pain of the wrong usually amounts to only a small fraction of the total hurt. After a while, it should become obvious to us that it is impossible to avoid being offended. However, the majority of our pain can be avoided if we will learn to deal with offenses rather than reliving them countless times. Failing to forgive others is a sure way of cutting the flow of God's power in our lives and yields a number of negative consequences. Before we examine these, let's look at some of the reasons why we may withhold forgiveness:

Reasons for Not Forgiving

We often fail to forgive others (and ourselves) because we don't think it's possible. We forget how God has graciously forgiven all of our sins through Christ's death, and rationalize why we can't forgive. These are some of the countless excuses we make for our unwillingness to forgive others and ourselves.

■ *The offense was too great.* Grant's wife had committed adultery, and he was bitter toward her. Her infidelity was too great a sin for him to forgive. But almost two years after the incident, God began to impress Grant with the idea that he should forgive his wife just as God in Christ also had forgiven him, completely and willfully. When Grant finally did forgive her, his forgiveness was coupled with a commitment to rebuild his relationship with her so that she would not be compelled to repeat the incident with someone else.

Roger sat shaking with anger as he recalled his wife's rape. His anger was destroying his health and his relationship with his wife. *How could any man, who really is a man, forgive such an act?* he wondered. The transient who had raped his wife had moved on, and in his perversion, had probably forgotten the incident. He never was caught. Continuing to allow the offense to produce bitterness might ultimately do more harm to Roger and his family than the destructive act of the rape.

■ *(S)he won't accept responsibility for the offense.* How many people have offended us but won't agree that they were at fault? The offense might be something slight, such as being overlooked at a social event, or something major, such as being emotionally neglected as a child. Having others agree that they've offended us isn't necessary for us to respond properly to their offense.

■ *(S)he isn't truly sorry.* John pulled a practical joke on you which caused you to be late for class, and your professor refused to accept your paper because you didn't have it in on time. John doesn't see anything wrong with a little joke—he's slightly sorry, but he still thinks it was hilarious. Even if John doesn't recognized the pain he's caused you, you still can extend forgiveness to him through Christ and refuse to hold the offense against him.

■ *(S)he never asked to be forgiven.* For whatever reason, the offender never got around to asking you for forgiveness. Are you going to withhold forgiveness until it's requested? Who is suffering, you or the offender? What would God have you do? (Read 1 Cor. 13:5 and Eph. 4:32.)

■ *(S)he will do it again.* Cheryl's husband had been out late every Friday night playing cards for three years. On some nights he didn't come home. "Me? Forgive that jerk?" Cheryl asked. The Lord said that the number of times we're to forgive is seventy times seven—in other words, regardless of the number of offenses. Forgiveness doesn't mean condoning or accepting unacceptable behavior. Some situations calling for forgiveness also require confrontation and/or allowing the offender to experience the consequences of his or her wrongful behavior. For Cheryl, failing to both forgive and confront her husband will cause her to be the bitter loser.

■ *(S)he did it again.* David had been a horrible husband to Mandy. However, after much effort, Mandy had forgiven him for his insensitivity, his greater concern for the guys on his softball team, his lack of affection for the children and his callous, domineering attitude. Then, David saw how poor his behavior had become. He began to change. His relationship with Mandy started to improve—until he stayed out late again with the guys. He had done it again! One mistake set the whole conflict back in motion.

■ *I don't like him(her).* Generally, we don't have a great deal of appreciation for those who have wronged us. In fact, every emotion within us may call for retaliation against the creep! Only when we realize that forgiveness is an act of the will, and not of the emotions, will we choose to forgive those who have hurt us.

■ *(S)he did it deliberately.* "He knew what he was doing, and he did it anyway!" George had been swindled out of ten thousand dollars by his "best friend," Hal. It had been a complex scheme which had required precise timing over a period of several months. As George sat stunned, his mind raced through those times he had been generous to Hal. He thought of how much he had loved Hal and had repeatedly trusted him. The swindle had been completely deliberate, and Hal had used him. George had been played for a sucker. Hal must be laughing at him now. Whether the offense was deliberate or not, God still wants George to forgive Hal.

■ *If I forgive the offense, I'll have to treat the offender well.* Ben excused his slander of Steve by pointing out how Steve had offended him. He felt justified in destroying Steve's reputation even though most of the things he had said about Steve were lies.

Shirley was cold to Greg, and had been for two weeks. It was her plan to punish Greg because he had offended her. She would forgive him all right—as soon as she was through punishing him.

■ *Someone has to punish him(her).* How often do we want God to be merciful to us and yet want Him to skin other people alive? When we don't see them suffer, we take it upon ourselves to be God's hand of vengeance.

Charles was their pastor, but according to Gloria, he had wasted the church's money. Gloria was in charge of the church women's group. She waited patiently for God to nail Charles, but when God didn't do what she thought He should, she just knew she was the divining rod for Charlie's back. Soon the church had taken sides—pro-Charles or anti-Charles. The result was that the church disgraced itself by splitting in hatred.

■ *Something keeps me from forgiving.* Satan actively promotes unforgivingness. When you attempt to deal with this problem honestly, you may be in for a tremendous spiritual battle, with both confusing and conflicting thoughts and emotions. Don't be surprised if you have to resist Satan at every turn in order to accomplish the task of forgiving the offender. Again, forgiveness is primarily an act of the will, not a warm feeling.

■ *I'll be a hypocrite if I forgive, because I don't feel like forgiving.* We often confuse hypocrisy with obedience. We are hypocritical only if we do something for selfish gain. For instance, a hypocrite might be a politician who comes to church in order to get its members to vote for him in the next election, but who despises the church and its people. To forgive as an act of the will in obedience to the Lord's command is true spirituality, not hypocrisy.

■ *I'll forgive, but I won't ever forget.* If we continue to harbor the memory of an offense, we are only fooling ourselves in thinking we have forgiven the offender, and we will not experience any freedom. In true forgiveness, we give up the right to remember an offense or to bring it up again during arguments. (Note: This doesn't mean that when we forgive a wrong, we'll never think of it again. But it does mean that we won't relish the memory. Choose to think about things that are *true, honorable, pure and lovely* [Phil. 4:8].)

■ *I'll forgive because I have found an excuse for the offense.* Hank had been very irresponsible during the early years of his marriage. His wife Sally had always been able to forgive him by placing the blame on his mother, who had babied Hank even after he was grown. Yet Sally was continually angered by Hank and his mother. In fact, her volatile temper was destroying her marriage.

Sally thought that she had forgiven Hank when she really had just excused him. By blaming Hank's mother for his immaturity, she had rationalized his behavior and had reduced her perception of his offensive actions like this:

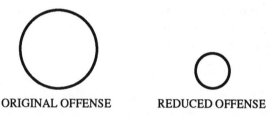

ORIGINAL OFFENSE   REDUCED OFFENSE

After reducing the offense, she then forgave it. The problem was that she did not deal with the real offense, but with a distortion of it. Therefore, the real offense remained intact in spite of her efforts at "forgiveness."

When you offend someone, or when someone offends you, do you immediately look for a "reason"? If you do, you may only be rationalizing. If you come up with an excuse for the question, *Why did I forgive him (or her)?* then you have not truly forgiven the offense. You have excused it.

Results of Not Forgiving

■ *Stress*: Living with the high level of tension brought by an unforgiving attitude in a relationship can result in a weakening of one's mental resources, emotional difficulties, physical exhaustion, and in some cases, illness.

■ *Self-Inflicted Reinjury:* Robert recalled this incident: "As I drove home, flashing into my memory was a guy I played basketball with in college. He was a great antagonist of mine, and was one of the few people

I have ever met whom I truly wanted to punch out. I began to remember the unkind things he had done to me. Soon, anger started creeping up inside me, and I realized that I had never forgiven him for what he had said and done those many years ago. Each time I would think of him, I would get a knot in my stomach and I'd be preoccupied with feelings of hurt and thoughts of revenge for hours, and sometimes, days." How many times are you reinjuring yourself because past offenses haunt you?

■ *No More Love:* "I don't know if I can ever love someone again" is a frequent complaint from those offended by a lover. Our deepest hurts come from those we love. One way we deal with the pain of being offended is simply to withdraw, refusing to love anymore. We often make this unconscious decision when we have not dealt with an offense adequately. We may desperately want to love again, but feel that we are incapable of it. Refusing to experience love and feeling unable to love are both devastating conditions.

■ *Bitterness:* Emotions trace their lines on our faces. We think others don't notice what's going on inside, but our anger can be detected by even the casual observer. One person recalled seeing a neighbor go through difficulties in her marriage. Hate created such an impression on her that her face became snarled. She still has an ugly look on her face. Withholding forgiveness produces ugliness of all sorts.

■ *Perpetual Conflict:* A couple, both of whom had been married previously, received counseling several years ago. Having been hurt in their first marriage, they anticipated hurt from their present spouse. At the smallest offense they each would react as if their spouse were about to deliver the final blow. They were constantly on the defensive, protecting themselves from the attacks they imagined their mate would deliver. Having been offended in the past, they anticipated more hurt in the present and future, and reacted in a way that perpetuated the conflict.

■ *Walls That Keep Others Out:* Strangely, many of us refuse the love that others want to give us. We often may become anxious and threatened when personal intimacy becomes possible.

Jane hoped and prayed that her husband Frank would come to know the Lord. This, she thought, would allow him to be more loving toward her and their children. One day, Frank accepted Christ and over time, his life began to change. He became interested in Jane, and started spending time with her and the children. He was sensitive and loving. Was it a dream come true? Instead of rejoicing, Jane deeply resented Frank for not changing sooner! *If Frank is able to love us like this now, then he's always had the ability,* she thought. She felt confused and guilty about her anger.

Jane's anger was a defense mechanism to keep distance between Frank and her. The closer they might get, the more pain she might experience if he reverted to his old ways.

She never had truly forgiven Frank, so the bricks of unforgivingness were stacked to form a wall that kept him from getting too close. Hiding behind a wall of unforgivingness is a lonely experience.

Summary of Reasons for Not Forgiving

1. *The offense was too great.*
2. *(S)he won't accept responsibility for the offense.*
3. *(S)he isn't truly sorry.*
4. *(S)he never asked to be forgiven.*
5. *(S)he will do it again.*
6. *(S)he did it again.*
7. *I don't like him(her).*
8. *(S)he did it deliberately.*
9. *If I forgive the offense, I'll have to treat the offender well.*
10. *Someone has to punish him(her).*
11. *Something keeps me from forgiving.*
12. *I'll be a hypocrite if I forgive, because I don't feel like forgiving.*
13. *I'll forgive, but I won't ever forget.*
14. *I have forgiven a lesser offense after excusing the real offense.*

Forgiveness Is Not Erasure

The modern idea of forgiveness is to approach an offense with a large eraser and wipe it off the books. God never has forgiven like this. He demanded full payment for each offense, the reason for the cross. Beside every offense on our ledger is the blood of Christ, which has paid for our sins in full.

The Christian has a unique capacity to extend forgiveness because he or she can appropriate the forgiveness of the cross. God has forgiven us fully and completely. We of all people know what it is like to experience unconditional forgiveness. As a result, we can forgive those around us. Think of it this way. *There is nothing that anyone can do to me (insult me, lie about me, annoy me, etc.) that can compare with the sins for which Christ has forgiven me.* When we compare the offenses of others to our sin of rebellion that Christ has completely forgiven, it puts them in perspective. In Eph. 4:32, Paul writes, *And be kind to one another, tender-hearted, forgiving each other, just as God in Christ also has forgiven you.*

List ten things for which you are glad God in Christ has forgiven you. This will prime you to be willing to forgive all other offenders.

1. _____   6. _____
2. _____   7. _____
3. _____   8. _____
4. _____   9. _____
5. _____   10. _____

The exercise on the following pages will help you to recognize any lack of forgiveness in your life and extend forgiveness to others as God in Christ has forgiven you.

■ Offense: Describe in some detail an event which caused you pain.

■ Persons to Be Forgiven: List everyone who participated in the offense.

■ Reasons for Not Forgiving: Go through the summary of reasons for not forgiving. Which ones apply?

■ Act of Forgiving: Choose to forgive, remembering the complete forgiveness you have in Christ.

■ At the conclusion of the exercise, use the prayer on page 208 (or use your own) as an exercise of faith for each offense.

Example:

Offense	Persons to Be Forgiven	Reasons for Not Forgiving	Date Forgiveness Was Extended
My brothers never had anything to do with me.	*Harry, Frank*	*The offense was too great; they didn't agree that they'd offended me; they never asked me to be forgiven; they'll do it again.*	*12-20-90*

• Offenses	• Persons to Be Forgiven

• Reasons for Not Forgiving	• Date Forgiveness Was Extended

Dear Lord,
I forgive _____ (name) *for* _____
(offense) *on the basis that God has forgiven me freely and has commanded me to forgive others. I have the capacity to do this because Christ has completely forgiven me. I do not excuse this person's offense in any way, nor do I use any excuse for not extending forgiveness. Thank You, Lord Jesus, for enabling me to forgive him (her).*

I also confess that I have sinned by using the following excuses for not forgiving:

Receiving Forgiveness

Having examined the importance of forgiving others, we must now ask, *What have I done to others that merits my seeking their forgiveness?* Step 4 has well prepared us for this step by enabling us to see *what* we've done wrong. Now we need to know *whom* we have wronged.

We are not yet ready to make amends with these people. Our task here is simply to list their names. In preparing this list, it may be helpful to use these guidelines, referring often to step 4:

- From whom did we cheat or steal?
- What promises and/or confidences did we break (sexual infidelity, lying, sharing something told to us in confidence) and whom did we hurt or betray?
- For whom did we cause pain by missing family obligations (birthdays, anniversaries) or other special days or commitments?
- What social responsibilities (laws, commitments) did we break or avoid, and who was harmed by this?
- What financial obligations did we avoid or wrongly create, and who was harmed or inconvenienced by our behavior?
- What have we done to harm those with whom we've worked?
- What physical damage—to either property or people—might we have caused by our eating-disordered behavior (refer to the "sanity list" in step 2 for help), and whom did we harm?
- To whom have we neglected to show gratitude?
- Who was victimized by our anger, resentment, blame or fear?

Persons We Have Harmed   **How We Harmed Them**

Motivations for Making Amends

There are many benefits we will receive from reconciling ourselves to others by making our amends with them. For one thing, it will release us from the control these people currently have on us. Think about those persons you have been avoiding; those whom you've been dodging, hoping they won't see you, or those you've been excluding from your circle of friends altogether. Have you ever considered that your guilt and fear are controls which are keeping you from the full enjoyment of life and love God desires for all who know Him?

To make amends is to be released from our relational past. It releases us from the fear of someone finding out something about us that we don't want them to know, a fear that will haunt and control us for the rest of our lives if unconfessed.

Making amends will enable us to enjoy increased fellowship with others, a key factor in our continued recovery. Isolation compelled us to continue our addiction; it went hand-in-hand with our eating disorder. Restitution frees us from that bondage.

Finally, as we take action to forgive others and experience their forgiveness, we will be able to forgive ourselves more completely. We will better understand that while our behavior may have been shameful, we as persons are not worthless. Learning how to love and forgive ourselves is a prerequisite for genuinely loving and forgiving others.

Read the Scriptures below and answer the questions that follow:

> *Therefore, since we have so great a cloud of witnesses surrounding us, let us also lay aside every encumbrance, and the sin which so easily entangles us, and let us run with endurance the race that is set before us,*
>
> *fixing our eyes on Jesus, the author and perfecter of faith, who for the joy set before Him endured the cross, despising the shame, and has sat down at the right hand of the throne of God.*
>
> Heb. 12:1-2

> *Do you not know that those who run in a race all run, but only one receives the prize? Run in such a way that you may win.*
>
> 1 Cor. 9:24

■ Understanding that a runner is more likely to win a race by facing forward throughout its duration, how will making amends enable you to be a better runner in the "race" of life?

■ What do you fear most about making amends?

• Do you think this is a realistic fear? Why or why not?

• Are you willing to lay this encumbrance of fear aside and make amends even though it may be painful to do so?

■ What possible joys might result from making amends?

■ To which of these do you most look forward, and why?

For Additional Reflection and Application

As we have mentioned, a prominent trait of eating-disordered behavior is perfectionism, and we ran a never-ending, self-defeating treadmill with our critical attitudes toward others, our constant weight-checks, our driven exercise sessions, our binging, purging and/or starving. But none of this ever did—or ever could—make us perfect! We only become perfect in God's eyes when we begin to comprehend His true nature, see how earnestly He desires that we receive His grace and forgiveness, and then learn to extend that forgiveness to others and ourselves.

Again, He has told us in Matt. 5:43-48 that when we forgive and love our enemies, we are made perfect—and if we are our own worst enemies, then we are the enemies who need God's forgiveness (and ours!) most.

■ Read John 8:1-11 and answer the following:
• What point was the crowd was trying to make to Jesus?

• From verse seven, did anyone in the crowd meet this criteria? If so, then who was it?

• Did this person claim that right? _____ What was that person's response?

• What does this passage tell us about forgiveness? Re-read it and think carefully, learning all you can about forgiveness.

Step Nine
My "Amended" Encounters

We make direct amends to such people
where possible, except when doing so will
injure them or others.

If therefore you are presenting your offering at the altar,
and there remember that your brother has something against you,
leave your offering there before the altar, and go your way;
first be reconciled to your brother, and then come
and present your offering.

Matt. 5:23-24

Those of us who have had an eating disorder are perfectionists in ways unique to us. Specifically, we tend to be overly-responsible about catering to the needs we perceive in others, sometimes even going so far as to assume responsibility for their sins! We each are somewhat like the person who read a "Help-Wanted" ad which specified, "only responsible persons need apply." He decided that this must be him, because no matter where he went, if anything went wrong, he was responsible!

This is why step 9 takes real discernment: As people with eating disorders, we tend to blame ourselves both for many bad things we have *not* done, and for those things that were not "bad" to begin with. Thus, we may find ourselves trying to "make amends" to some bewildered people whom we did not offend in the first place, or even stirring up trouble with others who were not aware of our offense but who, upon becoming aware, react quite negatively.

Step 9 may be another good place to seek help from our sponsors. Someone who is mature and familiar with our program of recovery can help us "check our thinking." Again, a sponsor should be someone whose relationship with God is more mature than our own. Ideally, this person will have spent a minimum of one year in recovery (preferably from eating disorders) and will have worked through the twelve steps, or at least through step 9. A person like this usually can provide the objectivity we need to determine whether or not amends need to be made, and if so, to whom.

Step 9 calls for *direct* amends. Direct not only means face-to-face; it means that we are open, honest and to the point, rather than seeking to excuse or minimize our wrongdoings, or attempting to manipulate a favorable response from the person with whom we are trying to make restitution.

Perhaps the most important point of step 9 is understanding that "making direct amends" does not refer only to making restitution with those we have wronged in the past, but learning how to be open, honest and straightforward in all of our relationships. We are not simply dealing with the past here; we are beginning to make a complete change in the way we relate to others, both in the present and the future.

Why is this necessary? Because part of our eating disorder has involved isolation, secrecy, private shame and seeking to manipulate others in order to seize and retain their approval. We manipulated our bodies to win or maintain the approval of others; we were relentless people-pleasers, never violating our unspoken "Charitable Noises Act," never telling others the truth when it needed to be told, stuffing and swallowing our emotions of anger and resentment, never really speaking up when we needed to—both for our benefit and for theirs. We continue to cringe at the word "confrontation," thinking that it means some brutal, ugly scene we want to avoid.

Let us then explore what *confrontation* really means:

■ Paraphrase the following passage:

> *Better is open rebuke than hidden love.*
> *Wounds from a friend can be trusted, but an enemy*
> *multiplies kisses.*
>
> Prov. 27:5-6, NIV

• Paraphrase:

• According to this passage, how would you define "friend" and "enemy"?

• Why would a person sacrifice telling the truth, or being open and direct with another person?

The truth of the matter is, most of us are afraid that we will lose the acceptance we crave from others if we are confrontive. We are afraid that we will be perceived as "attacking" the person if we are open, honest and direct with him or her. We therefore need to learn what it means to *confront*, as opposed to *attack*, because these words have very different meanings.

> *If your brother sins against you, go and show him his fault, just between the two of you. If he listens to you, you have won your brother over.*
>
> Matt. 18:15, NIV

■ RULE NUMBER ONE: ALL CONFRONTATIONS MUST HAVE A GOAL.
- According to the above Scripture, what is the *goal* of all confrontations, in general terms?

■ RULE NUMBER TWO: ALL CONFRONTATIONS MUST HAVE A FOCUS.
- According to the above Scripture, what is the general *focus* of all confrontations?

■ RULE NUMBER THREE: SOMEONE HAS TO INITIATE A CONFRONTATION; CONFRONTATIONS DO NOT INITIATE THEMSELVES.
- According to the above Scripture, who should initiate a confrontation: the one who committed an offense, or the one who was offended?

■ RULE NUMBER FOUR: CONFRONTATION BEGINS BETWEEN A CERTAIN NUMBER OF CERTAIN PARTICULAR INDIVIDUALS.
- According to the above Scripture, what persons should be involved in the initial confrontation?

■ Given the above guidelines and Scripture references, what would be your working definition of *confrontation*?

Consider this definition: *A confrontation occurs when one goes to a person who has committed an offense against him, draws attention to the offense (without accusing or attacking the offender), and makes it plain that he seeks to enlist the cooperation of the offender to resolve the issue(s) or problem(s), with a goal toward building and strengthening the relationship. It involves acting in love (because love rejoices in the truth* [1 Cor. 13:6]) *and accepting the wrongdoer while revealing the unacceptability of his performance.*

Models for Confrontation

Wrong Way

- Goal: *Dave really hurt me when he said those nasty, rotten things to me. I want him to be really sorry for that! If I let him know how hurt I am, then he will hurt, too.*

- Focus: *I really want to hurt Dave. He is a bad person because of what he did!*

- Initiator: *I will give Dave the "cold shoulder" and the "silent treatment," while telling everyone else how much he hurt me. Then he'll come crawling, and beg my forgiveness.*

- Players: *Dave, me and anyone else I can whine to and get on my side, so that Dave can have M.H.P. (Maximum Humiliation Potential).*

- Conclusion: *Hurt Dave so badly that it will kill our relationship. Who needs him, anyway?*

Right Way

- Goal: *Dave said some things which really offended me. I'm hurt. I don't hate him, but I need to resolve this with him for the sake of our relationship.*

- Focus: *I want to be open, honest and direct with Dave, and I especially want to find out if I might have contributed in some way to this problem. I want to concentrate on the offense, not attack Dave.*

- Initiator: *I want to go to Dave right away. He may not even know that he's offended me, or if he does, he might want to take steps with me to repair our relationship.*

- Key Players: *This is just between Dave and me. If I complain to other people, I will only damage Dave's reputation and offend him for sure! Just in case, though, I will talk this out with my* (counselor/sponsor/ someone else who is objective and uninvolved), *just to make sure I'm doing the right thing.*

■ Conclusion A: *Dave and I talk about the matter. After pointing out what happened and its impact on me, he learns about an area of sensitivity in my life and apologizes. I may learn about some important issues between us, about which I was previously unaware.*

■ Conclusion B: *Dave says that he doesn't want anything more to do with me, and that he wanted to hurt me in the first place. I'm hurt by the loss of this relationship, but am aware that God loves me deeply, is fully pleased with me, totally accepts me and that I am absolutely complete in Christ. This knowledge will help me to pursue new relationships confidently and enable me to forgive Dave (although I may never see him again).*

Surprised by Conclusion B? We need to remember that relationships are risky, even though they are good. People can reject us—and we can reject them! We are not obligated to like other people any more than they are obligated to like us. Something we may have failed to learn long ago, which led us to manipulate others to try to win their approval, is that we cannot do anything to *make* others like us! When we perform to win others' approval, then they approve of our performance, not us.

Our future encounters need to be "amended," governed by healthy patterns of relating, instead of by our old eating-disordered game plans.

Try the new pattern for yourself:

- Offense:

- Goal:

- Focus:

- Initiator

- Key Players:

We will not explore the conclusion until you actually have carried out the game plan. You see, we cannot control the outcome of the situation, even by "doing the right thing"! We only can approach the issue in a manner which is healthy, both for the other person and for us. The days of manipulating others by "doing the right thing" need to be over. Our actions can contribute to a desired outcome, but we cannot control the decisions of others. We need to accept their decisions—just as we want them to accept our decisions without controlling us!

Words to Avoid in Confrontation

Although we cannot control the decisions and responses of others, we can use care to avoid accusatory language. Two words to avoid are *why* and *you*. Each of these is almost guaranteed to prompt a defensive reaction. "Why did you hurt me!?" should become, "When you did that, I thought you were trying to hurt me, and when I thought that, I felt angry." Remember, it is not the event itself that produces our emotions, but how we evaluate the event based on our beliefs and thoughts. We are responsible for our feelings; others cannot *make* us feel a certain way. But our hurt feelings (which are legitimate) do warn us that something is wrong and needs to be resolved.

A Suggested Outline for Confrontations

- *What I heard (saw) you say (do) was . . .*
- *What I thought when you said/did that was . . .*
- *What I felt when I thought that was . . .*
- *What I want now is . . .*
- *What I will do to help is . . .*

The first statement is merely an observation—which we state in order to avoid making an accusation. The second statement is a declaration of our thoughts about the matter; we state our conclusions in order to investigate them further. In the third statement, we simply describe our emotional response (making very clear use of "feeling words" like, *happy, sad, glad, mad, afraid,* etc.). In the fourth statement, we announce the change we hope to see in the other's behavior, words or attitude. Here, we are declaring ourselves to be allies, rather than taskmasters, who are willing to help facilitate change, while recognizing that a person's behavior/words/attitudes are his or hers, not ours to dictate or control.

A Final Word About "Amends-ments"

Being honest, open and direct of course applies to making amends when we have wronged another person. While we were engaged in eating-disordered behavior, we may have wronged others by obstinate pride, control, secrecy, lying and avoidance through passive-aggressive retaliation (giving others the "silent treatment," procrastinating, gossiping, hurting ourselves to inflict pain on others). Sometimes we need to go and "fess up" to these persons, and be willing to make *restitution,* or "right our wrongs." (For example, some of us will find it necessary to go to the grocery store from which we stole and pay for our stolen merchandise).

In such cases, our choice is clear: We need to take our list of those we have wronged, which we developed in step 8, and seek out appropriate ways to make restitution to them. This may involve making certain acts of restitution (paying back or returning money or goods, etc.) or simply "coming clean" with the persons we have harmed, admitting that we were wrong, that we sinned against them and that we want to apologize and ask their forgiveness.

No, it doesn't appeal much to pride to go "hat-in-hand" to those whom we have wronged, admit our wrongdoing, apologize and seek to make amends to them. But again, pride is part of our problem, and we will do well to let it die as God changes our ways of thinking, feeling and acting. We need to continue to seek healing in our relationships—whether by objectively discussing how another person has offended us or how we have offended him or her. In so doing, it is most important that we seek and accept God's forgiveness of us, and that we be willing to forgive ourselves.

So from now on we regard no one from a worldly point of view. Though we once regarded Christ in this way, we do so no longer.

*Therefore if anyone is in Christ he is a new creation;
the old has gone, the new has come!*

*All this is from God, who reconciled us to himself
through Christ and gave us the ministry of reconciliation:*

*that God was reconciling the world to himself in
Christ, not counting men's sins against them. And he has
committed to us the message of reconciliation.*

*We are therefore Christ's ambassadors, as though
God were making His appeal through us . . . .*

2 Cor. 5:16-20, NIV

When we pursue healthy ways of viewing ourselves and relating to others, we defeat the thought patterns which led to our eating-disordered behavior. Step 9 enables us to continue the process of learning how to turn outward rather than inward. It reinforces the knowledge that we don't have to be anxious about whether or not others believe we are okay, because we are completely accepted by God. This enables us to continue relating to others with the knowledge that we *are* okay, even without their approval. Finally, by seeking reconciliation and healing through healthy confronting, we continue learning how to contribute both to our own lives and to the lives of others. What a privilege God has given us in step 9!

Step Ten
My "Surrendered Serenity" Continues

***We continue to take personal inventory,
and commit to agree with the truth about
ourselves and act upon it.***

Therefore let him who thinks he stands take heed lest he fall.

1 Cor. 10:12

Let's recap a bit.

In step 1 we acknowledged that we had a problem which was controlling us, and that this problem was making our lives chaotic and unmanageable. In step 2 we acknowledged the existence of God—a power greater than ourselves—and conceded that He alone could restore us to sound judgment. We became willing to let Him change us in step 3 by giving our lives over to His care. In step 4 we "cleaned house," acknowledging some of the self-defeating patterns of sin that had governed our lives. In step 5 we "'fessed up" to what we had learned about ourselves in step 4, disclosing to another person the things about ourselves that we had kept hidden and secret in the past. We submitted our inventory to God in step 6, asking Him to remove patterns of sin from our lives. In step 7 we asked God to replace our false-belief systems—which governed both our thought patterns and our chaotic lives—with the truth of His Word. We listed those with whom we needed to make amends for past misdeeds in step 8, and in step 9, carried that further by not only addressing those whom we'd offended, but by learning to change the way we typically relate to others, especially in matters requiring confrontation.

Now in step 10, we courageously take an exciting step—BACKWARD! *Oh please, not again! Inventory again? Surely, we don't have to relive the past again. After all, this is real life, not a science-fiction story, right?*

Wrong. Well, right and wrong. Yes, this is real life, and no, we do not necessarily need to retread ground we already have covered. But we need to understand that going forward means continuing to take responsibility for ourselves—as faithful stewards of the lives God has given us—aware that the old patterns of sinful, dysfunctional thinking and behavior which characterized our lives in the past can re-surface. We therefore need to monitor these on a daily basis as a form of maintenance.

Step 10 is an outline for a daily inventory which will give us information about at least two things: (1) Destructive patterns of behavior which are re-emerging from the past, and which we want to discontinue; (2) New patterns of behavior which are emerging, and which we want to continue. The latter allows us to rejoice in the good news that we are growing, and that new things are happening to and through us as a result of God's work within us!

New Fruit Flavors

In the fifth chapter of Galatians, Paul lists the new fruit which should characterize our new lives in Christ. Often, these are erroneously referenced as "fruits" of the Spirit. Actually, *fruit* is singular, not plural. Just as an apple has different parts—stem, core, seeds, flesh, outer skin, taste, smell—so too, our new lives in Christ have different parts—love, joy, peace, patience, kindness, goodness, faithfulness, gentleness, self-control (Gal. 5:22-23, NIV), but comprise one whole fruit (*me!*). Let's examine these parts individually:

Love
Literally, *agapeh*—used in the Greek New Testament for God's love—is the unconditional acceptance and desire for the highest good of another, which results in fair, honest and open styles of relating.

Joy
Joy is derived from the word, *chara*, which means gladness and gratitude. As we see the positive changes God is making within us; as we see that we can lead healthy lives; and as we see healing in our relationships, our thinking begins to reflect that which is known in twelve-step programs as an "attitude of gratitude." We become grateful for life, instead of viewing it as a burden.

Peace
Literally, *eireneh*, from which we get the name "Irene," *peace* means tranquility, harmony, concord, exemption from rage. Peace results from confronting the source of our anger appropriately, not lashing out at others or inwardly at ourselves (see step 4, "Constructive Anger"). We also gain

peace when we learn to accept and tolerate others, especially in relation to those differences about them that we cannot change.

Patience

Patience is derived from *makrothumia*, which means perseverance, endurance, constancy, long-suffering, not vengeful. Simply put, patience means to "hang in there!" Sometimes we get anxious because we cannot control what is happening; in the past, anxiety usually meant BINGE TIME! Patience means that we endure, not by naively pretending that a situation of hardship is under control, but by understanding and acknowledging that even though we are not in control, God is.

Kindness

Literally, *chrestotes*, meaning moral goodness, integrity, benevolence. Exercising kindness means doing those things which are most loving. That does not mean "being nice." *Being nice* means, "manipulating others by our own behavior so that they always will like us." When we truly love someone, we consider his or her highest good, not whether he or she always will like us. Thus, we seek to be open, honest, direct—you know, all that step-9 stuff! Sometimes kindness hurts, but it never harms.

Goodness

From the word, *agathosuneh*, or uprightness, this means to have moral integrity, an earnest desire for God to lead us into patterns of thinking and relating which are loving, honest and open, and for which we need never be ashamed.

Faithfulness

Literally, *pistis*, which means believing, persuaded, trusting. We need to ask God daily to increase our faith and trust in Him, and to help us grow and mature in that faith and trust, no matter what our circumstances or feelings about them might be.

Gentleness

Originally, *prautes*, meaning meekness, not weakness. To be gentle means to draw back from being impulsive in anger or given to a raging response, and instead consider our response thoughtfully, not with a goal to retaliate, but to resolve the problem.

Self-Control

Oh, how our eating-disordered thinking loved to corrupt this one! Literally, *egkrateia* means possessing the strength to govern one's self. From where does this "strength" come? Remember, our relentless efforts at maintaining control by self-will gave us an eating disorder! It made our lives chaotic and unmanageable. God gives us power to manage (not control) our lives appropriately, making us faithful, responsible stewards of our attitudes and actions. This means that we allow Him to call the shots, and submit ourselves to His authority through accountability to Him (by knowing, following and living out His Word) and to others (by their feedback, which we process with them).

We have explained the fruit of the Spirit because a step-10 inventory is, in part, the means by which we daily tend to its growth and cultivation in our lives. In addition, it is a tool for maintaining our daily health with regard to our eating disorder—a "finger on the pulse," so to speak. Such maintenance requires that we be attentive to our emotions (instead of stuffing and avoiding them) and take care that we are not isolating ourselves and withdrawing from others.

Keeping a Journal

Initiating and maintaining a journal is an important part of treatment and recovery from eating disorders. Identifying potential triggers for relapse (see step 2), as well as developing a strategy for dealing with relapse, should be a part of this exercise. The journal should include the following:

- Types/amounts of food eaten in normal meals during the day.
- Types/amounts of food eaten during a binge.
- Time/place a normal meal is taken.
- Time/place we binge or purge.
- Thoughts and feelings before, during and after eating a normal meal.
- Thoughts and feelings before, during and after a binge or purge episode.

A journal should not include a record of body weight or caloric consumption, but behavioral strategies to both prevent relapse and deal with relapse should one occur.

General Tips

■ *First-two-bites rule:* Generally, we taste only the first two bites of any food. To help prevent binging, eat the first two bites of every food slowly and completely, rolling it around the tongue and learning to describe each taste sensation. This will slow your eating and eventually result in your thinking of food as *food*, not as a *feeling*.

■ *Eat at scheduled mealtimes and in only one particular area, never in front of the TV or in a work or other area.*

■ *Avoid keeping a list of "forbidden foods."* "Forbidding" certain foods makes them all the more enticing and triggers the urge to binge. It is better to allow yourself small portions of "forbidden" foods in a planned way, in conjunction with regular meals.

■ *Include in each meal representative portions from all basic food groups.* Consult a dietician, if necessary. If you are in treatment, this can (and should) be arranged for you. If it has not been arranged, speak up!

■ *Eat at a table, with proper utensils, from a plate or bowl, not from serving dishes or packages.*

■ *Pray before you eat.* Ask God to help you cultivate an "attitude of gratitude" for His provision.

■ *Check your weight no more than once a week.*

■ Include the following in your journal:

  • *What have I learned today . . .*
    * *about the world?*
    * *about God?*
    * *about others?*
    * *about life?*
    * *about myself?*
  • *How have I felt today at different times?*
  • *What do I feel good (bad) about having done today?*
  • *How have I been kind (unkind) to myself today?*
  • *How have I been honest (dishonest) with others today?*
  • *What have I accomplished (failed to accomplish) today?*

- *If any unfinished business remains from today, have I turned it over to God, knowing that I will return to it tomorrow, according to His will?*

The Importance of Our Emotions

The outline suggested for your journal (above) includes some general questions about feelings. However, because learning how to deal with our emotions appropriately is essential to recovery, we'd like for you to consider incorporating a more specific inventory of your emotions into your journal as well.

You may recall that in step 7, we learned that our emotions often comprise our reactions to immediate events. However, our emotions are also products of our family backgrounds, past experiences, relationships and patterns of responses. Some of us have a tendency to despise our emotions, believing that it was our feelings that prompted our eating-disordered behavior in the first place. Many of us come from homes where we were not loved and affirmed as children. As a result, we may have learned to repress painful emotions because we didn't want to believe that something was wrong with our families, our source of stability and security. If we were abused as children, we may have become numb, unable to feel either anger or joy, hurt or love. Some of us have developed a habit of forgetting painful events as a defense mechanism. There are many different ways to block pain in our efforts to gain a sense of value and control, but we need to begin reversing this trend by tuning in to our feelings and finding someone who will encourage us to be honest about them. We can then use our feelings as a gauge to determine if our response to a situation is based on the truth or a lie.

It is important to realize that feelings are neither right nor wrong. It is what we do with them that determines "sin" or "obedience." Emotions are signals which tell us something about our environment. Only people on TV with pointed ears can get by without them! We need to be honest about our feelings so that they can tell us what we need to know about our perceptions, and we need to learn how to respond to them with *egkrateia*, or self-control, the last item on the "Fruit of the Spirit" list.

In order to be attentive to our feelings, it is helpful to cultivate a list of "feeling words" and understand what they mean. Below is a partial listing:

- *Anger:* (indignation, irritation, annoyance, rage)
- *Anxiety:* (uneasiness, intense fear, panic)
- *Ashamed:* (embarrassed, humiliated, feeling foolish)
- *Depression:* ("the blues," sadness, worthlessness)

- *Fear:* (alarm, timidity, apprehension)
- *Happiness:* (pleasure, contentment, joy, gladness)
- *Inadequate:* (insufficient, lacking)
- *Resentment:* (unresolved anger, desire to punish)
- *Sad:* (sorrowful, melancholic, mournful)
- *Shame:* (hopelessness, low self-esteem)

You will need to understand these and other emotions as you experience them. This will take time. As a start, try using this brief, easy plan in your journal.

■ *Recognize*
- Describe your situation.
- Describe your response to the situation: your feelings, thoughts and actions.

Example: Ask yourself: *What am I feeling? How many of the "feeling words"* (from the list above) *am I experiencing right now? What is happening that is causing me to feel this way? What are these feelings suggesting I do?* Also ask yourself: *What am I thinking about? What am I trying to avoid? What are my thoughts?*

(Note that the question, *What am I thinking about?* is an inquiry about the *focus* of your thoughts; *What are my thoughts?* is an inquiry about the *content* of your thoughts.)

■ *Reject*
- Which false belief(s) are you believing?
    * *I must meet certain standards to feel good about myself* (fear of failure).
    * *I must be approved* (accepted) *by certain others to feel good about myself* (fear of rejection).
    * *Those who fail are unworthy of love and deserve to be blamed and condemned* (fear of punishment/propensity to punish others).
    * *I am what I am; I cannot change; I am hopeless* (shame).

■ *Replace*
- Identify the truth from God's Word that applies to the situation:
    * **Justification:** *God has forgiven me completely; therefore, I am fully pleasing to Him, despite my performance* (Rom. 3:19-25; 2 Cor. 5:21).

* **Reconciliation:** *I am totally accepted by God; therefore, I don't need the approval of others to have a sense of value* (Col. 1:19-22).
* **Propitiation:** *I am deeply loved by God. Because Jesus bore the punishment for mankind on the cross, I don't need to punish others or myself* (1 John 4:9-11).
* **Regeneration:** *I am absolutely complete in Christ. Because of His renewing work in me, I can change. I need never be ashamed.* (2 Cor. 5:17).

■ *Respond*

Look over the list comprising the fruit of the Spirit below. Choose any of those which would be a healthy response to your circumstances and emotions. Ask God to provide what you need to respond appropriately.

* *Love:* unconditional acceptance and desire for the highest good of another.
* *Joy:* gladness and gratitude.
* *Peace:* tranquility resulting from resolved anger; acceptance, tolerance.
* *Patience:* persevering; exercising endurance, long-suffering.
* *Kindness:* Doing those things that contribute to the highest good of another.
* *Goodness:* exercising moral integrity in our thoughts and behavior.
* *Faithfulness:* trusting in God despite unwelcome feelings or circumstances.
* *Gentleness:* seeking resolution (not retaliation) with others.
* *Self-Control:* Submitting ourselves to God for strength to govern our lives appropriately, in accordance to His Word.

This is a simple plan, but a complex process which takes time and work! PLEASE DO NOT EXPECT TO MASTER THIS IMMEDIATELY! After having spent a lifetime of avoiding emotions through compulsive behavior, simply learning how to identify and understand painful feelings is a tremendous feat in itself! Our eating disorder was part of our strategy to avoid knowing and dealing with our feelings, circumstances and behaviors responsibly. Looking at ourselves closely is new, awkward and often painful for us. However, as we accustom ourselves to doing this on a regular basis, we gradually will come to enjoy the growth, maturity and health it produces. In the meantime, we need to be patient with ourselves and allow ourselves opportunities to grow through successes and failures.

Relapse Intervention

The panic button has been pressed—whether by rejection, poor performance, threat of failure, an unkind word or deed—and I am on my way to a binge and/or purge. This is my emergency, self-intervention protocol. THIS IS NO DRILL! This is a real emergency!

Sponsor's Name: **Phone:**
Pastor's Name: **Phone:**
Recovering Friend: **Phone:**
Other Source of Help: **Phone:**

IF I CANNOT GET A RESPONSE FROM ANY OF THE ABOVE (PEOPLE ARE NOT RESPONSIBLE FOR MY BEHAVIOR), REFER TO MY "FEELINGS LIST" SO FAR. BEGIN WRITING:

- *What am I feeling right now?* List the emotions.
- *What is today's weather situation?*
- (For women) *What day is it in my monthly cycle?*

Unpleasant feelings are an indication of unmet needs or expectations in our lives.

- Look again at your list of feelings. Try to identify the need behind each one.
- Now, look to those needs. Is there someone (more than one) who can facilitate meeting some of those needs? List name(s).
- Get his/her (their) phone number(s) and contact that person (or persons).
- Repeat the "Serenity Prayer" (see page 237). How does it apply here? What can you change, and what do you need to surrender to God?
- Work your program!
- Read your Bible! Read Ps. 91. (Keep a marker there and read it often, especially in times of trial.)
- Read *The Search for Significance*!
- Check your phone directory for a listing of support-group meetings (such as O.A.); see if one is in progress NOW, and GO!
- Repeat "The Declaration" (see page 193) and think about what it means!
- Find someone else who might need help and offer to help!

Why is all of the above necessary? An old adage in twelve-step groups is, "If you fail to plan, you plan to fail." Again, our eating disorder was part of our strategy for avoiding the prospect of facing ourselves honestly and confronting problematic issues in our lives squarely. Taking inventory is new and awkward for us; we have become far more skillful at "barking up the wrong tree" than we have at examining ourselves. By keeping up with our feelings and monitoring our lives by taking a regular inventory, we can continue to grow into and enjoy the health God desires to give us.

Step Eleven
My Journey into Renewing Life

**We learn to grow in our relationship with Jesus Christ
through prayer, meditation and obedience,
seeking His wisdom and power to live according to His
will as He reveals it to us.**

*But if any of you lacks wisdom, let him ask of God,
who gives to all men generously and without
reproach and it will be given to him.
But let him ask in faith without any doubting, for the one who
doubts is like the surf of the sea driven and tossed by the wind.*

James 1:5-6

Jesus Christ's primary purpose in allowing Himself to be made human, to be made sin and to be crucified on our behalf was to reconcile us to God. He desires to have a relationship with us. In John 10:1-4, 14, He said:

> *Truly, truly, I say to you, he who does not enter by the door into the fold of the sheep, but climbs up some other way, he is a thief and a robber.*
> *But he who enters by the door is a shepherd of the sheep.*
> *To him the doorkeeper opens, and the sheep hear his voice, and he calls his own sheep by name, and leads them out.*
> *When he puts forth all his own, he goes before them, and the sheep follow him because they know his voice . . . .*
> *I am the good shepherd; and I know My own, and My own know Me . . . .*

In Scripture, Jesus is often described as the *good shepherd*, who is faithful to lead and provide for His sheep, those who are His. The point of this passage is clear: We can't hope to follow Jesus unless we know His voice, and we can't distinguish His voice from any other until we have cultivated an intimate relationship with Him. Such a relationship takes time, but God clearly wants it. He has taken the initiative in having a relationship with us.

> *We love because He first loved us.*
>
> 1 John 4:19

> *By this the love of God was manifested in us, that God has sent His only begotten Son into the world so that we might live through Him.*
> *In this is love, not that we loved God, but that He loved us and sent His Son to be the propitiation for our sins.*
>
> 1 John 4:9-10

Not only has God taken the initiative to have a relationship with us, but He has given us the resources we need to enjoy that relationship: His Holy Spirit, His Word (the Scriptures) and prayer.

Prayer is our opportunity to communicate through the Holy Spirit to God. Scripture is God's Word (the final authority on matters of life) communicated through His Spirit to us.

Concerning the Holy Spirit's involvement in our communication with God, Scripture says:

> *And in the same way the Spirit also helps our weakness; for we do not know how to pray as we should, but the Spirit Himself intercedes for us with groanings too deep for words . . . .*
>
> Rom. 8:26

> *. . . for through Him we . . . have our access in one Spirit to the Father.*
>
> Eph. 2:18

> *But know this first of all, that no prophecy of Scripture is a matter of one's own interpretation,*
> *For no prophecy was ever made by an act of human will, but men moved by the Holy Spirit spoke from God.*
>
> 2 Pet. 1:20-21

Prayer

As we have just read, the Holy Spirit intercedes for us in prayer. Some people hold to the premise that this means speaking to God in a *tongue,* or language that may be known only to God. But the Holy Spirit isn't limited in the ways He can speak to God on our behalf. To "pray in the Spirit" is to pray with His guidance and wisdom, with an open mind which allows Him to place on our hearts those people and things we need to speak to God about.

Many people experience a problem when it comes to prayer—literally! They don't pray until they experience a problem. This approach is what some have called "foxhole religion." A soldier, stuck in a foxhole on a battlefield, bullets flying, makes grandiose promises to God which he swears he'll keep if God will just get him out of the battle safely.

This phenomenon is terribly unfortunate. Prayer is not the bargaining or vending-machine process many of us have come to think of it as being. Neither is it an exercise in futility. Consider the following:

"Prayer"

Master, they say that when I seem
To be in speech with you,
Since you make no replies, it's all a dream
—One talker aping two.

They are half right, but not as they
Imagine; rather I
Seek in myself the things I meant to say,
And lo! the wells are dry.

Then, seeing me empty, you forsake
The Listener's role, and through
My dead lips breathe and into utterance wake
The thoughts I never knew.
And thus you neither need reply
Nor can; thus while we seem
Two talking, Thou art One forever, and I
No dreamer, but Thy dream.[1]

Elements of Effective Prayer

Prayer, then, is not the process of "sending out thoughts into the void," but again, the means by which we have communication with God. We *praise* Him in prayer, not because He needs our praise (see Ps. 50:7-15), but because we need the humility which accompanies acknowledging God as *God* (not us, with our relentless "I-dolatry," for which one act of worship was our eating disorder). We present our *petitions*, or requests, to Him in prayer as well, with the understanding that we need to give Him our concerns and the burdens of our hearts, and trust Him to do what is best for us. (Refer to step 3, regarding turning our lives—all of our needs and concerns—over to God through Jesus Christ.) Think about this poem:

"Broken Dreams"

As children bring
Their broken toys
With tears for us to mend,
I brought my broken dreams to God
Because He was my Friend.

But then instead
Of leaving Him
In peace to work alone,
I hung around and tried to help
With ways that were my own.

At last I snatched
Them back, and cried
"How can You be so slow?"
"My child," He said,
"What could I do?
"You never did let go."

(Unknown)

Another part of prayer is *thanksgiving*. Again, thanking God is a way of acknowledging that He is God. It also is a part of our "attitude of gratitude," which results from the new things He is making possible in our lives. Gratitude is, in fact, a wonderful experience and quite a suitable alternative to pride.

Trusting is another aspect of prayer. We confirm our trust in God by verbalizing to Him our decision to trust Him and keep His Word. The real distance between head knowledge and heartfelt faith can be measured by the distance from our will to our lips—what we are willing to commit to God and/or others through the spoken word.

This is not "name it and claim it" theology, which seeks to use spoken words as magic talismans to make the universe conform to our wants; in other words, "Christianized Control!" But our spoken words do have great power (James 3:5, 9-10), and we can use them in positive ways by committing ourselves to God's Word and by affirming others and ourselves with truth.

Finally, prayer involves *sharing*; that is, sharing the concerns and burdens of others, as well as sharing God's thoughts. This latter form of sharing occurs when we are willing to quiet and still ourselves before the Lord.

■ Paraphrase the following passage:

> *The Lord Almighty is with us; the God of Jacob is our fortress.*
>
> *Come and see the works of the Lord, the desolations he has brought on the earth.*
>
> *He makes wars cease to the ends of the earth; he breaks the bow and shatters the spear, he burns the shields with fire.*
>
> *"Be still, and know that I am God; I will be exalted among the nations, I will be exalted in the earth."*
>
> Ps. 46:7-10, NIV

• Paraphrase:

• What is the target for God's "desolations"?

• God's command to "Be still..." literally means to "cease striving." What does this mean to you?

• What instruction do you receive from this passage in terms of prayer?

■ Most twelve-step groups make reference to the Lord's Prayer:

> *Our Father who art in heaven, hallowed be Thy Name.*
> *Thy kingdom come. Thy will be done, on earth as it is in heaven.*
> *Give us this day our daily bread.*
> *And forgive us our debts, as we also have forgiven our debtors.*
> *And do not lead us into temptation, but deliver us from evil. For Thine is the kingdom, and the power, and the glory, forever. Amen.*
>
> Matt. 6:9-13

• Where do you see *praise* in the Lord's Prayer?

• Where do you see *petition*?

• Where do you see *thanksgiving*?

• Where do you see *trusting*?

• Where do you see *sharing*?

Did you have difficulty with any of the above questions? You should have! Prayer is not a formula. The elements of praise, petition, thanksgiving, trusting and sharing are not always a part of every prayer. Our compulsive, addictive thinking wants—demands!—a nice neat formula to "get it right." When we pray, whether our prayer is liturgical or spontaneous, we need to open our hearts to God. Yes, again, openness, honesty and directness are our necessary tools for cultivating a meaningful relationship with God, just as they are necessary for meaningful relationships with others. Jesus said, *Yet a time is coming and has now come when the true worshipers will worship the Father in spirit and truth, for they are the kind of worshipers the Father seeks. God is spirit, and his worshipers must worship in spirit and in truth* (John 4:23-24, NIV).

Let's consider another prayer, popular in twelve-step groups—this time, as it was originally written:

"Prayer for Serenity"

God, grant me the serenity
To accept the things I cannot change,
The courage to change the things I can,
And the wisdom to know the difference;
Living one day at a time, enjoying one moment at a time,
Accepting hardship as a pathway to peace;
Taking, as Jesus did, this sinful world as it is,
Not as I would have it.
Trusting that You will make all things right
If I surrender to Your will,
So that I may be reasonably happy in this life
And supremely happy with You forever in the next. Amen.[2]

And here is still another:

Prayer of St. Francis of Assisi

Lord make me an instrument of your peace
Where there is hatred, let me sow love
Where there is injury, pardon
Where there is doubt, faith
Where there is despair, hope
Where there is darkness, light
Where there is sadness, joy.

O Divine Master, grant that I may not so much seek
To be consoled, as to console
To be understood, as to understand

To be loved, as to love.

For
It is in giving that we receive
It is in pardoning that we are pardoned
It is in dying that we are born to eternal life.[3]

■ What do you notice about prayer by reading the well-known prayers above?

• What principles, regarding a spiritual approach to life, do you see in these prayers?

■ Step 11 refers to "seeking His wisdom and power to live according to His will as He reveals it to us." How do the above prayers relate to this aspect of step 11?

■ Compose a simple prayer of your own, thinking about the typical elements of prayer (praise, petition, thanksgiving, trusting, sharing), the Lord's Prayer, the Prayer for Serenity and the Prayer of St. Francis of Assisi:

Meditation

Like prayer, meditation also is a problem for many, conjuring up to modern Western minds images of a guru-like person in a lotus position, levitating above the ground. Thus, the Christian, with the current paranoia about "New-Age" practices, may become suspicious at the mere mention of *meditation.*

However, meditation is a biblical word and concept. Here are some examples of various words and meanings used to describe meditation in the Old and New Testaments, which clarify its meaning for the Christian.

Old Testament
- *Hagah* (Gen. 24:63; Josh. 1:8; Ps. 1:2; 63:6; 77:12; 143:5; Is. 33:18): This Hebrew word means to murmur, to ponder. This would seem to indicate that meditation is to be both a mental and a verbal process.
- *Siyach* (Ps. 104: 34; 119:15, 23, 48, 78, 148): To ponder, to converse, muse, complain. *Siyach* also involves a combination of thinking and speaking—and even a little griping, maybe!
- *Hagiyg* (Ps. 5:1): to murmur, complain.
- *Higgaown* (Ps. 19:14): solemn murmuring.
- *Haguwth* (Ps. 49:3): musing.
- *Sychach* (Ps. 119:97, 99): reflection or devotion.

New Testament
- *Promeletao* (Luke 21:14): to premeditate, to meditate before.
- *Meletao* (1 Tim. 4:15): to imagine, to revolve in the mind.

What is *meditation?* Based on all the above, a conclusive, working definition for the Christian is, *a cognitive process of understanding and evaluation to resolve issues and problems, utilizing the resources of thinking, conversing, planning/anticipating and imagining, for the purposes of spiritual devotion, development and enrichment.*

Christians can meditate alone or with others, sharing insights and concerns, developing strategies for dealing with issues of growth and development for the whole person, and can even use their imaginations to rehearse complaints and dislikes.

Let's try a simple exercise in meditation, using Psalm 1. Remember, we will use our resources of thinking, imagining, talking to others and ourselves—and even complaining, if needed—(with resolution as our goal) as we meditate.

■ To read Psalm 1 for meditation, find someplace quiet to sit and relax. Begin with this prayer, remembering that meditation involves devotion:

Lord Jesus, I want to grow in my relationship with You by meditating on Your Word in these moments. As I meet with You in this way, I pray that I may receive wisdom and power to carry out Your will and plan as You reveal them to me. Help me to be nourished and refreshed by Your Spirit during this meditation, and draw me closer to Yourself and Your healing power.
In Your Name, Lord Jesus, I pray.   Amen.

• Begin by reading the passage aloud, slowly. Highlight or circle words which may stand out to you, for whatever reason.

Psalm 1, NIV

(1)   *Blessed is the man who does not walk in the counsel of the wicked or stand in the way of sinners or sit in the seat of mockers.*
(2)   *But his delight is in the law of the Lord, and on his law he meditates day and night.*
(3)   *He is like a tree planted by streams of water, which yields its fruit in season and whose leaf does not wither.Whatever he does prospers.*
(4)   *Not so the wicked! They are like chaff that the wind blows away.*
(5)   *Therefore the wicked will not stand in the judgment, nor sinners in the assembly of the righteous.*
(6)   *For the Lord watches over the way of the righteous, but the way of the wicked will perish.*

• Think about the phrase, "counsel of the wicked." *Counsel* means to teach by asking questions and allowing others to draw, from their own answers, conclusions that the counselor wants the counselee to draw. When we walk in the counsel of the wicked, what are we doing?

• Describe what you imagine when you see the phrases, "stand in the way of sinners" and "sit in the seat of mockers."

- What are your feelings as you think about these things?

- In view of the above two questions, what does the phrase, "blessed is the man," mean to you?

- When have you found yourself "walking in the counsel of the wicked" or "standing in the way of sinners" or "sitting in the seat of mockers"?

- What does verse two suggest as an alternative and a corrective to the hazards described in verse one?

- What do you think *meditate* means here?

- What is the meaning of "day and night" as it is used here?

- Imagine yourself as a "tree planted by streams of water." Is this an appealing picture to you? Why or why not?

- What does the psalmist say is the advantage this type of tree enjoys?

- Why does this tree have these advantages?

- Why do you think the person whose "delight is in the law of the Lord," and who "on his law meditates day and night," is likened to this type of tree?

- *Chaff* refers to unusable husks of grain, such as wheat, which are separated from usable grain during threshing and winnowing (beating the grain out of the husk, and then blowing off and scattering the unusable hulls by letting the wind carry it away). Imagine as best you can the threshing and winnowing process, and write down why you think the psalmist uses this as an illustration of the wicked.

- Paraphrase verses five and six.

- Now, *premeditate* (promeletao). What good counsel do you glean from this passage as a strategy for your life?

- Read the following and compare it with Ps. 1:2.

> *Hearing that Jesus had silenced the Sadducees, the Pharisees got together.*
>
> *One of them, an expert in the law, tested him with this question:*
>
> *"Teacher, which is the greatest commandment in the Law?"*
>
> *Jesus replied, "'Love the Lord your God with all your heart and with all your soul and with all your mind.'*
>
> *"This is the first and greatest commandment.*
>
> *"And the second is like it: 'Love your neighbor as yourself.'*
>
> *"All the Law and the Prophets hang on these two commandments."*
>
> Matt. 22:34-40, NIV

- Read Ps. 1:2 again. What is the point of verse two, and what does it mean to you?

- Think about Ps. 1 and consider anyone with whom you might share your insights. Pray again the prayer you used on page 240.

Making Time for God

One of the biggest obstacles to our personal relationship with God is T-I-M-E.

Many of us resist approaching God because we feel like we owe Him a large chunk of our time. We do "owe" everything to God, but not in the same sense that we would "owe" another person. God has paid our debts! Our response to Him is simply gratitude—again, an "attitude of gratitude"— for demonstrating His care for us by sending His only Son to die in our place, and for giving new life to others and to us.

It is important to understand that because God loves us, He is delighted with any effort we make to spend time with Him, and especially if it means having to say no to something else in order to keep the appointment.

These are some suggestions for pursuing time alone with God:

- *Start slowly, but be consistent.* You may want to spend ten minutes with God each day at first. You can read ten verses of Scripture, and spend the rest of your time in prayer. The point is, do it every day.
- *Make an appointment with God and keep it.* Set aside one special time each day, reserved specifically for you and God.
- *Find a quiet place.* Take the phone off the hook if necessary.
- *Choose a time when you'll be free of interruptions.* If you like the morning hours, but know that on one particular day you will be interrupted, do not be "married" to the morning. Set it up for a later time in the day, when you do not anticipate an interruption.
- *Ask the Holy Spirit for help and guidance.* God wants to meet with you, too! Ask the Holy Spirit for assistance to have this time with Him.

Every relationship takes time. God, more than anyone else, knows this. As you continue to grow with Him, you'll find yourself wanting to spend more time with Him. And you'll gain a special blessing in knowing that God isn't just everyone else's God, but yours.

Step Twelve
My New Life with Others

Having had a spiritual awakening, we try to carry the message of Christ's grace and restoration power to others with eating disorders, and to practice these principles in all our affairs.

All this is from God, who reconciled us to himself through Christ and gave us the ministry of reconciliation . . . and he has committed to us the message of reconciliation. We are therefore Christ's ambassadors, as though God were making his appeal through us.

2 Cor. 5:18, 19b, 20, NIV

A Spiritual Awakening?

God created us in His own image, to be like Him. God is loving and giving, reaching out in love to us without controlling, manipulating or coercing us. It follows, then, that we are our healthiest when we are involved in reaching out in ministry to others, without trying to manipulate or control them to meet our own needs. Our spiritual awakening begins when we ask Jesus Christ to be the Savior and Lord of our lives (step 3). The goal of that awakening, or new beginning, is to become willing to care for others and reach out to them as God does us.

We must be quite clear in our understanding of what this means. We are *not* "fourth persons of the Trinity," so we cannot expect to give infinitely, in codependent fashion. Unlike God, we are finite. We can *save* no one, but we can *help* someone. Learning that delicate balance is difficult— especially for those of us whose lives have been governed by the chronic performing and "people-pleasing" tendencies characteristic of eating-disordered behavior—but it is possible.

Acquiring this sense of balance requires our having a spiritual awakening. This includes learning humility by recognizing our own limitations and trusting that because God extends to us His love, grace and constant availability, He will meet our needs sufficiently. We therefore do

245

not need to continue operating by our old patterns of controlling and perfectionistic behavior. A spiritual awakening also includes a realization of the wonderful news that we no longer have to search for purpose, worth, meaning and security through overly-dependent relationships, our career, performance, compulsions, addictions or causes.

"Spiritual Awakenings" and "New Creations"

> *So from now on we regard no one from a worldly point of view. Though we once regarded Christ in this way, we do so no longer.*
> *Therefore, if anyone is in Christ, he is a new creation; the old has gone, the new has come!*
> *All this is from God, who reconciled us to himself through Christ and gave us the ministry of reconciliation.*
>
> 2 Cor. 5:16-18, NIV

■ How have you thought of yourself from a "worldly point of view" in the past?

• How have you tended to view others?

• How have you tended to view Christ?

■ According to the above passage, what changes can you expect in the way you perceive . . .
  • yourself?

  • others?

• God?

■ What is the result of being a "new creation" in relationships with others, according to this passage?

• What is the connection between this result and the statement, ". . . carry the message of Christ's grace and restoration power to others with eating disorders" in step 12?

Carrying the Message

Helping others is, in part, the telling of a story, the story of our progress toward health through the Twelve-Step program. In the spaces below, write:

■ How the Twelve-Step program has deepened your faith in Jesus Christ:

■ How the power of Jesus Christ is transforming your life:
• Emotionally:

• Relationally:

• Spiritually:

- Mentally:

- Physically:

■ Describe any differences in your behavior that have resulted from identifying false beliefs and replacing them with the truths of God's Word:

■ Have other people noticed changes or improvements in your behavior? If so, describe some of these changes:

By writing down some of the many changes that have occurred in your life since you entered recovery, you are gathering some good material to share with those who are new to the program. Scripture gives us many helpful hints for successful sharing. Let's look at some of these:

■ Read Gal. 6:1. How would you try to restore someone with an eating disorder in a "spirit of gentleness"? Give several possible applications of this instruction:

- What can you do to ensure that helping another person won't be the cause of a downfall in your own life? List several possible safeguards:

■ Read Phil. 1:27; 4:8-9. Is our example to others as important as what we say to them? Explain:

As we experience the joys of giving comfort to others with eating disorders, and as we mature in our own relationship with God, we will begin to be compelled to share His transforming love and power with those who are outside the program as well. This is the work of the Holy Spirit, yet some of us shy away from this responsibility because we fear rejection. And for good reason! Christ has assured us of being rejected by at least some people when we take a stand for Him.

In John 15:18-25, Jesus said that the reason we are rejected is because, indeed, we are His: *If you belonged to the world, it would love you as its own. As it is, you do not belong to the world, but I have chosen you out of the world. That is why the world hates you* (John 15:19, NIV). Almighty God has chosen us! He has made us new, set us apart and reconciled us to Himself. We are special and precious to Him, but we should not expect the world to be thrilled with our commitment to Christ.

Sadly, we often forget that we are special and chosen. At times, we wish we belonged to the world. When faced with the choice of being rejected for taking a stand for Christ or going along with the world, we often choose the world. The fear of rejection is too great. But God has given us a solution to the fear of rejection! We no longer have to accept the opinions of others as the basis of our significance. Instead, the love and acceptance of the infinite, Almighty God frees us to live unreservedly for Him. We can step out in faith and lovingly tell people about Christ's offer of forgiveness. Billions of people are waiting to hear His message!

Proclaiming His Excellencies

God has set us apart to be the light and salt of the world, and His Spirit enables us to powerfully influence those around us for all eternity. We have the ability to see the world's spiritual poverty through God's eyes and offer to it God's magnificent solution.

■ Read Eph. 2:10 and 1 Pet. 2:9. What is the result of being specifically chosen by God?

■ Read Luke 19:10. What was Jesus' goal in coming to earth?

■ Read Matt. 4:19; 28:18-20. As we yield our lives to Him and the truth of His Word, in what will we inevitably be involved?

■ Reflect on what Christ has done for you. Make a list of as many things as possible. Then make a parallel list of what was true of you before you trusted in Christ:

In Christ   **Before Christ**

■ Read 1 Cor. 6:19-20 and 2 Cor. 5:14-15. How does your perception of what Christ has done for you affect your motivation to communicate the gospel to others?

■ How does your perception of the lost condition of those without Christ affect your desire to share your faith?

■ Read John 17:18; Acts 1:8; Rom. 1:14-16 and 2 Cor. 5:18-20. What is your personal role in evangelism?

■ Read Eph. 6:19 and 1 Pet. 4:11. What is the Holy Spirit's role in evangelism?

■ Read Ex. 4:7-12; Is. 50:4; 61:1; Rom. 9:14-16. What do these passages tell you about God's responsibility for the salvation of people?

■ In what practical ways can you apply these teachings?

Practicing These Principles . . .

■ Paraphrase the following passage:

> *Once, having been asked by the Pharisees when the kingdom of God would come, Jesus replied, "The kingdom of God does not come with your careful observation,*
> *"nor will people say, 'Here it is,' or 'There it is,' because the kingdom of God is within you."*
>
> Luke 17:20-21, NIV

• Paraphrase:

■ Compare the above with the following passage:

> *So do not worry, saying, "What shall we eat?" or "What shall we drink?" or "What shall we wear?"*

*For the pagans run after all these things, and your
heavenly Father knows that you need them.
But seek first his kingdom and his righteousness, and
all these things will be given to you as well.*

Matt. 6:31-33, NIV

• Each of these passages says something important about *the kingdom of
God*. Combine the two messages into one thought and write it in the
spaces below.

• These passages also say something important about *anxiety and worry*.
Combine the two messages into one thought and write it in the spaces
below.

■ Sometimes people assume a "Santa-Claus" view of God from these
passages, but that is not their intent. Whenever reading the Bible, keep
in mind the principle: "Always let Scripture interpret Scripture." Again,
consider the above passages with the following:

*Do not be anxious about anything, but in everything,
by prayer and petition, with thanksgiving, present your
requests to God.
And the peace of God, which transcends all
understanding, will guard your hearts and your minds in
Christ Jesus.*

Phil. 4:6-7, NIV

• Obviously if someone is anxious, simply saying, "Don't be anxious!"
is not helpful. What does this passage really mean when it says, "Do not
be anxious"?

■ Thinking about all of the above passages, what should we assume about ourselves in reference to our circumstances? (Let this answer be your own "theology of dealing with adversity.")

There are many times when we encounter problems, stressful situations or painful, even traumatic events, and God not only helps us get through them, but moves us into much better circumstances and surroundings. Unfortunately, even when these are the results, we may remain bitter or continue to harbor resentment because the "bad guy" doesn't get punished. We may continue to be angry about how the negative circumstances came about, or we may find any number of other ways to remain "peevish."

Perhaps our attitude parallels that of the woman whose son was drowning: She dropped to her knees and cried out, "Oh please God, save my little boy! Please, oh please, God, don't let him drown."

Suddenly the waves parted, and the water came up as if it were a giant hand and gently carried the boy to deposit him, safe and sound, at his mother's feet. His mother's response to this was, "Well, God, he was wearing a hat when he fell in, You know!"

Practicing twelve-step principles involves incorporating those principles into our thoughts and behavior on a day-to-day basis. It means acknowledging powerlessness in difficult situations, believing in God's power to make us sane, turning ourselves and our circumstances over to Him and so forth.

Let's look at a picture of how this might work:

You are at work, trying to complete a project which is due that day. You have invested a tremendous amount of time and effort on this project, and are looking forward to its completion.

As you access your computer file, you discover that a fellow employee unwittingly downloaded and lost all of your work. When you do your best to confront him according to the guidelines in step 9, the employee takes a very nonchalant attitude, seems unconcerned and "blows it off." Your boss is very unhappy and does not care that the misfortune is not your fault. She lets you know that the project is still due, and that your job may be hanging by a thread. Your other co-workers seem equally unconcerned about your problem. None offer to help, and all have excuses why they are not able to help when you ask them for assistance.

You stay very late at the office. When you finally leave to go home, you find that a parking ticket is on your car, that one of your tires is flat and that you do not have a spare. You look across the street and see "Porky's Twenty-Four Hour Doughnut and Pastry Emporium." You run in panic to the public pay phone to call your sponsor, only to look inside "Porky's" and see your sponsor eating doughnuts.

■ Apply step 1 to every point in the above scenario to which you think it applies:

• Do the same with step 2:

• Do the same with step 3:

• Apply the "Prayer for Serenity" to the above scenario (see page 237). What are the "things you cannot change"?

• What things can you change?

- What might the phrase, ". . . accepting hardship as a pathway to peace" mean here?

- Apply the Scripture passages from Matthew, Luke and Philippians (see pages 251-252) to the above scenario.

- Cite other steps from your workbook which also apply to the above scenario and describe how they apply.

The "Great Commission" is the invitation Christ gives us to be a part of His reaching out to others. Because He made us, He knows that we will be at the height of good health when we grow out of our self-centeredness and into ministry (reaching out) to others. This is what He said . . .

> *"All authority in heaven and on earth has been given to me.*
> *"Therefore go and make disciples of all nations, baptizing them in the name of the Father and of the Son and of the Holy Spirit,*
> *"and teaching them to obey everything I have commanded you. And surely I am with you always, to the very end of the age."*
>
> Matt. 28:18-20, NIV

As we share the principles of recovery and the Person of Jesus Christ with others, we notice some important points in this command. Jesus said that His is the authority under which we are to go. Biblically, *authority* is not controlling others (Luke 22:24-30), but learning to serve, help and support others as they exercise stewardship over their lives.

When we travel from state to state on the highway, we encounter traffic laws which may vary according to terrain, density of population, types of roads and many other circumstances. However, we need to follow those laws, not because of someone's need to control us, but because our safety and well-being, as well as that of all others on the road, are greatly facilitated by our submission to that helpful, protecting authority.

This illustrates the authority of Jesus. We do not earn His favor by our obedience (we already have His favor!). Rather, we submit to His authority and obey Him because His commands are given for our safety and contribute to the well-being of others and ourselves.

It is because of the goodness of His authority that He commissions us to live our lives at their healthiest and fullest by cultivating mature relationships with others and by reaching out to them in ministry. The job He gives us is one of teaching. "Making disciples" literally means "making students," or teaching others by word and example the blessings of His authority in our lives, and the life He gives as we . . .

- admit our powerlessness.
- come to believe in Him.
- turn our lives over to His management.
- courageously make an inventory of our lives.
- confess our sins to Him and to another person.
- allow Him free rein in changing the patterns of our lives.
- seek Him to renew our minds and transform us.
- face the wrongs we have committed against others, and become willing to make amends to them.
- amend the patterns of our lives which are destructive to our relationships with others.
- continue to take inventory of ourselves.
- grow in relationship to Him by prayer and meditation.
- reach out to others in and with His healing love and grace.
  . . . knowing that *He is with us always, to the very end of the age!*

The Twelve Steps give us a framework, a guide, for life and health in Jesus Christ. But it is He Himself who is the source of health, the Giver of Life. The Twelve Steps, then, point us toward Him. We must recognize that although we can assist others in their spiritual awakening, He alone is the One who saves—*Jehovah Rapha*, the Lord who heals. In our helping, we both draw the attention of others to Him, and experience the strength and health which God intends for us as we extend His love to others.

A Note to Group Leaders

Rapha's Twelve-Step Program for Overcoming Eating Disorders has been written to meet the requirements for treatment in both inpatient and outpatient settings, as well as for Rapha's *Right-Step Program.* Although much of this workbook's focus is directed toward individual initiative and activity in resolving eating-disordered behavior, groups will find marked results when the content of this workbook is combined with leadership and training materials from the *Right-Step Program.*

Although this workbook makes little distinction between the anorexic, bulimic and compulsive overeater, groups with a high number of participants may find it helpful to make a distinction between people with different types of eating disorders. This is because of subtle differences in the obsessional thought processes unique to each eating disorder. Therefore, the "best of all worlds" would be a separate group for each disorder. If numbers do not make this arrangement possible, placing compulsive overeaters in one group, while combining those with anorexia and bulimia would be best. (Those with anorexia and bulimia typically share the same obsession with body weight and image, whereas compulsive overeating, with its absence of purgative behavior and weight gain, features an obsession with self-medication through eating.)

Group leaders as well as group members will also benefit significantly by reading and working through *The Search for Significance* book and workbook by Robert S. McGee. Much of the material in this workbook reflects its influence and content, making a separate study of *The Search for Significance* an effective adjunct to twelve-step work.

We welcome your feedback and input! For more information about Rapha's *Right-Step Program,* write to Rapha. Other comments and inquiries may be addressed to:

RAPHA, INC.
P.O. Box 580355
Houston, TX 77258
or
Wm. Drew Mountcastle, M.A., LPC
Jennings and Associates
1100 N.W. Loop 410 Suite 301
San Antonio, TX 78213

Suggested Reading

Addiction and Eating Disorders

Alcoholics Anonymous. 3d. Ed. New York: Alcoholics Anonymous World Services, Inc., 1976.

Also called *The Big Book,* this book contains many helpful insights about the nature and manifestations of dependency, the Twelve Steps of Alcoholics Anonymous, and personal stories from the founders and pioneers of A.A.

Christian, Shannon with Margaret Johnson. *The Very Private Matter of Anorexia Nervosa.* Grand Rapids, MI: Zondervan, 1986.

Shannon is the wife of Christian song writer and singer, Chris Christian. Her book is a good chronicle of the development of the obsessive thinking associated with anorexia. It also focuses on recovery issues.

Halvorson, Patricia A., Ph.D. and Patricia A. Neuman, Ed.S. *Anorexia Nervosa and Bulimia: A Handbook for Counselors and Therapists.* New York: Van Nostrand Reinhold Company, 1983.

This is the definitive handbook for people in helping professions who work with eating disorders, including therapists, nurses, doctors, social workers, even volunteers interested in working in this field. It includes practical helps for facilitating treatment and recovery, including forms and paperwork, and gives steps on how to organize a community-based therapy group for eating disorders.

L., Elisabeth. *Twelve Steps for Overeaters: An Interpretation of the Twelve Steps of Overeaters Anonymous.* San Francisco: Harper/Hazelden, 1988.

This book is not written from a Christian perspective, but nonetheless gives valuable insight into the application of the Twelve Steps for compulsive eating and for creating a new relationship with food altogether.

May, Gerald C., M.D. *Addiction and Grace.* San Francisco, CA: Harper and Row Publishers, 1988.

Written by a psychiatrist who has worked extensively in dependency issues, this book explores the concept of addiction—to anything—as an

261

attempt to assert control over our lives. Presents the theological and spiritual concepts of God's grace as the means toward human freedom.

O'Neill, Cherry Boone. *Starving for Attention*. New York: Continuum, 1982.

The oldest daughter of singer and actor, Pat Boone, places particular emphasis on family and control issues in her struggle with anorexia nervosa. Cherry is a good example of the anorexic who engages in bulimic-like binging and purging, but who still would be classifed as anorexic. Hers is an upbeat story, nonetheless, because of its ultimate emphasis on recovery.

Spickard, Anderson, M.D. and Barbara R. Thompson. *Dying for a Drink*. Waco, TX: Word Books, 1985.

Especially geared for the Christian community, this book offers valid case histories with clinical facts about addiction. Spickard is a professor of medicine and director of the division of the Vanderbilt Institute for Treatment of Alcoholism.

Springle, Pat. *Codependency*. 2d ed. Houston and Dallas, TX: Rapha Publishing/Word Inc., 1990.

A Christian perspective which identifies primary and corollary characteristics manifested by *codependents*, persons struggling with the adverse effects of dysfunctional relationships. Provides illustrations and questions which allow the reader to discover the cause of codependency, its relationship to our real needs, common biblical misinterpretations and the process of spiritual renewal through sound biblical principles.

The Twelve Steps of Alcoholics Anonymous. New York: Harper/Hazeldon, 1987.

While this book is not written from a Christian standpoint, it does offer a series of helpful, short discussions that elaborate on interpretations of the Twelve Steps.

Vath, Raymond E., M.D. *Counseling Those with Eating Disorders*. Waco, TX: Word Books, 1986.

This is the fourth volume in Word's *Resources for Christian Counseling Series*, edited by Gary Collins, Ph.D., and is written by Cherry Boone O'Neill's psychiatrist. Dr. Vath explains the origins and results of eating disorders and also focuses on confronting perfectionism, self-esteem, sexual identity, depression, control, "the deception factor" and dependency in eating disorders as they relate to treatment.

Relational

Allender, Dan B., M. Div., Ph.D. *The Wounded Heart. Hope for Adult Victims of Childhood Sexual Abuse.* Colorado Springs, CO: NavPress, 1990.

Sexual abuse is a frequent issue for those who are subject to eating disorders. An abuse victim himself, Allender discusses the dynamics and damage of abuse, and outlines biblical prerequisites necessary for growing into relationships with God and others characterized by loving honestly, boldly and rightly.

Hancock, Maxine and Karen Burton Mains. *Child Sexual Abuse: A Hope for Healing.* Wheaton, IL: Harold Shaw Publisher, 1987.

Karen Mains is known for her "Chapel of the Air" radio program, and Maxine Hancock is a respected author. Together, they examine the painful issue of sexual abuse, especially as it occurs in the Christian community. A comprehensive study, this book examines the offender and family issues, as well as focusing on issues of the survivor's acceptance and forgiveness of him- or herself.

Johnson, James E., D.Min. *Freedom from Depression.* Plainfield, NJ: Haven Books, 1980.

Dr. Johnson is a member of the National Association of Christians in Social Work and the National Association of Social Workers (NASW), as well as former director of Social Services at Philhaven Hospital in Lebanon, Pennsylvania, adjunct professor of counseling at Evangelical School of Theology in Myerstown, Pennsylvania and director of the Worship Center Counseling Center in Lebanon, Pennsylvania. Chronic depression usually accompanies eating disorders; Dr. Johnson explores how to recognize and deal with it from a Christian perspective.

_____. *The Gift of a Sound Mind.* Scottdale, PA: Herald Press, 1980.

Dr. Johnson describes how we can obtain a "sound mind" from God to change how we view ourselves and relate to others responsibly. His book includes an approach to self-discipline that is characterized by a godly perspective, instead of control.

Love, Patricia, Ed.D., with Jo Robinson. *The Emotional Incest Syndrome: What to Do When a Parent's Love Rules Your Life*. New York: Bantam Books, 1990.

The problem of enmeshment between a parent and eating-disordered offspring is an all-too-familiar dynamic in the E.D. family. Though she is not writing from a Christian perspective, Dr. Love has written a valuable examination of enmeshment which bears much consideration in dealing with family issues in recovery from eating disorders.

McGee, Robert S., Jim Craddock, and Pat Springle. *Your Parents and You*. Houston and Dallas, TX: Rapha Publishing/Word, Inc., 1990.

A book and workbook which illustrates the many ways parents shape our self-concepts, our perceptions of God and our relationships with others. Offers practical ways to reshape false perceptions using the truth of God's Word.

Napier, Augustus, Ph.D., with Carl A. Whitaker, M.D. *The Family Crucible*. New York: Bantam Books, 1978.

Doctors Napier and Whitaker provide an interpretive look at a dysfunctional family system by following one family through the course of family therapy. Included is an easily-understandable explanation of the family as a system.

Thorkelson Rentzel, Lori. "Emotional Dependency: A Threat to Close Friendships." San Rafael, CA: Exodus International-North America, Box 2121, 94912.

A booklet primarily for those with a tendency toward unhealthy dependency in same-sex relationships. Identifies root causes of emotional dependency and characteristics of dependent relationships, with practical and spiritual suggestions for freedom.

White, John. *Eros Defiled: The Christian and Sexual Sin*. Downers Grove, IL: InterVarsity Press, 1977.

A counselor and associate professor of psychiatry at the University of Manitoba examines the many forms of sexual defilement which have been prevalent since the Fall of Man. A caring, compassionate book.

Wilson, Earl D. *A Silence to Be Broken.* Portland, OR: Mulnomah Press, 1986.

Dr. Wilson is a psychologist in private practice in Portland, Oregon, and has gleaned excellent observations and devised important interventions for understanding and dealing sexual abuse. This book includes information for understanding offenders and "A Prayer for Healing" for the abuse survivor.

Theological and Devotional

Chambers, Oswald. *My Utmost for His Highest.* Westwood, NJ: Barbour and Co., Inc., 1963.

A daily devotional which, upon every reading, offers new insights as the Christian grows in faith.

Lewis, C.S. *Mere Christianity.* New York: Macmillan Publishing Co., 1943.

Lewis, a staunch atheist prior to his conversion, writes a Christian apologetic for the half-convinced whose intellect may be an obstacle to faith.

Little, Paul. *How to Give Away Your Faith.* Downers Grove, IL: InterVarsity Press, 1966.

A practical book on the methods and dynamics of personal evangelism.

_____ . *Know Why You Believe.* Downers Grove, IL: InterVarsity Press, 1967.

An examination of critical issues concerning Christianity which enable the reader to sort the facts that provide solid ground for belief.

Parham, A. Philip. *Letting God: Christian Meditations for Recovering Persons.* San Francisco: Harper and Row Publishers, 1987.

Dr. Parham is an Episcopal priest and is on the board of directors of the National Episcopal Coalition on Alcohol. This book is a daily devotional guide for Christians based on the Twelve Steps of Alcoholics Anonymous and includes Scripture and prayer for each devotional entry.

Phillips, J.B. *Your God is Too Small.* New York: Macmillan Publishing, 1961.

Phillips holds that many of us are crippled by a limiting idea of God. He discusses some of these limitations, and then examines the broad, all-encompassing reality of God.

Robertson, Pat, with Bob Slosser. *The Secret Kingdom: A Promise of Hope and Freedom in a World of Turmoil.* Toronto: Bantam Books, 1984.

Pat Robertson, founder of Christian Broadcasting Network, Christian journalist and one-time presidential hopeful, has written an excellent study of what he refers to as "laws" by which the kingdom of God works, including the "law of reciprocity," the "law of use," the "law of perseverance," the "law of responsibility," the "law of greatness," the "law of unity," the "law of miracles" and the "law of dominion."

Tippet, Sammy. *The Prayer Factor.* Chicago, IL: Moody Press, 1988.

Help for establishing a consistent, effective prayer life through a fresh understanding of the gift and power of prayer.

Notes

Introduction
1. Springle, Pat, *Codependency*. 2d ed. (Houston and Dallas, TX: Rapha Publishing/Word, Inc., 1990), p. 23.
2. Copyright © by *The A.A. Grapevine, Inc.*, from a card which includes the Twelve Steps and the Twelve Traditions of A.A., published by A.A. World Services, Inc., P.O. Box 459, Grand Central Station, New York, NY 10163.

Step 1
1. Kubler-Ross, Elisabeth, *On Death and Dying* (New York: MacMillan Publishing, 1969).

Step 2
1. Robert S. McGee, Jim Craddock and Pat Springle, *Your Parents and You* (Houston and Dallas, TX: Rapha Publishing/Word, Inc., 1990, adapted from p. 9 with permission.
2. Ibid, pp. 191-194.
3. Ibid, pp. 195-197.
4. Ibid, pp. 199-201.
5. Ibid, pp. 203-206.
6. Ibid, pp. 207-210.
7. Ibid, pp. 231-236.

Step 3
1. McGee, Craddock and Springle, *Your Parents and You,* pp. 245-272. Reprinted and adapted by permission.
2. John Rippon, "How Firm a Foundation," 1787.

Step 4
1. Charles Stanley, *Forgiveness,* (Nashville, TN: Oliver-Nelson Books, 1987), p. 16.
2. Mary Bevis and Nini Sieck, "Bless Your Heart Each New Day," *Samplers from the Heartland,* © 1987.
3. Ibid.

4.   John White, *Eros Defiled: The Christian and Sexual Sin* (Downers Grove, IL: InterVarsity Press, 1977), p. 10.
5.   C.S. Lewis, *God in the Dock: Essays on Theology and Ethics.* Edited by Walter Hooper. (Grand Rapids, MI: William B. Eerdmans Publishing Co., 1970), p. 124.

Step 5

1.   *The Book of Common Prayer* (New York: The Church Pension Fund, 1945).
2.   Charles Wesley, "And Can it Be that I Should Gain?" stanzas 4-5. Source: *Hymns II*, (Downers Grove, IL: Inter-Varsity Christian Fellowship of the United States of America, 1976), p. 88.

Step 6

1.   Pat Springle, *Codependency*, adapted from pp. 142-143 with permission.
2.   Erwin W. Lutzer, *How to Say No to a Stubborn Habit* (Wheaton, IL: Victor Books, 1979), pp. 21-23.

Step 7

1.   *The New College Latin and English Dictionary* (Toronto: Bantam Books, 1981), p. 176.

Step 11

1.   C.S. Lewis, *Poems.* Edited by Walter Hooper. (New York: Harcourt, Brace and World, Inc., 1964), p. 122.
2.   Reinhold Niebuhr, "The Serenity Prayer." (St. Meinrad, IN: Abbey Press).
3.   *The Twelve Steps of Alcoholics Anonymous* (New York: Harper/ Hazeldon, 1987), p. 128.